PIE

Edible

Series Editor: Andrew F. Smith

EDIBLE is a revolutionary series of books dedicated to food and drink
that explores the rich history of cuisine. Each book reveals the global
history and culture of one type of food or beverage.

Already published

Apple Erika Janik, *Avocado* Jeff Miller, *Banana* Lorna Piatti-Farnell, *Barbecue*
Jonathan Deutsch and Megan J. Elias, *Beans* Nathalie Rachel Morris, *Beef* Lorna
Piatti-Farnell, *Beer* Gavin D. Smith, *Berries* Heather Arndt Anderson, *Biscuits and
Cookies* Anastasia Edwards, *Brandy* Becky Sue Epstein, *Bread* William Rubel,
Cabbage Meg Muckenhoupt, *Cake* Nicola Humble, *Caviar* Nichola Fletcher,
Champagne Becky Sue Epstein, *Cheese* Andrew Dalby, *Chillies* Heather Arndt
Anderson, *Chocolate* Sarah Moss and Alexander Badenoch, *Cocktails* Joseph M.
Carlin, *Coconut* Constance L. Kirker and Mary Newman, *Coffee* Jonathan Morris,
Corn Michael Owen Jones, *Curry* Colleen Taylor Sen, *Dates* Nawal Nasrallah,
Doughnut Heather Delancey Hunwick, *Dumplings* Barbara Gallani, *Edible
Flowers* Constance L. Kirker and Mary Newman, *Edible Insects* Gina Louise Hunter,
Eggs Diane Toops, *Fats* Michelle Phillipov, *Figs* David C. Sutton, *Foie Gras*
Norman Kolpas, *Game* Paula Young Lee, *Gin* Lesley Jacobs Solmonson,
Hamburger Andrew F. Smith, *Herbs* Gary Allen, *Herring* Kathy Hunt, *Honey* Lucy
M. Long, *Hot Dog* Bruce Kraig, *Hummus* Harriet Nussbaum, *Ice Cream* Laura B.
Weiss, *Jam, Jelly and Marmalade* Sarah B. Hood, *Lamb* Brian Yarvin, *Lemon* Toby
Sonneman, *Lobster* Elisabeth Townsend, *Melon* Sylvia Lovegren, *Milk* Hannah
Velten, *Moonshine* Kevin R. Kosar, *Mushroom* Cynthia D. Bertelsen, *Mustard*
Demet Güzey, *Nuts* Ken Albala, *Offal* Nina Edwards, *Olive* Fabrizia Lanza,
Onions and Garlic Martha Jay, *Oranges* Clarissa Hyman, *Oyster* Carolyn Tillie,
Pancake Ken Albala, *Pasta and Noodles* Kantha Shelke, *Pickles* Jan Davison,
Pie Janet Clarkson, *Pineapple* Kaori O'Connor, *Pizza* Carol Helstosky,
Pomegranate Damien Stone, *Pork* Katharine M. Rogers, *Potato* Andrew F. Smith,
Pudding Jeri Quinzio, *Rice* Renee Marton, *Rum* Richard Foss, *Saffron* Ramin
Ganeshram, *Salad* Judith Weinraub, *Salmon* Nicolaas Mink, *Sandwich* Bee Wilson,
Sauces Maryann Tebben, *Sausage* Gary Allen, *Seaweed* Kaori O'Connor, *Shrimp*
Yvette Florio Lane, *Soda and Fizzy Drinks* Judith Levin, *Soup* Janet Clarkson,
Spices Fred Czarra, *Sugar* Andrew F. Smith, *Sweets and Candy* Laura Mason,
Tea Helen Saberi, *Tequila* Ian Williams, *Tomato* Clarissa Hyman, *Truffle* Zachary
Nowak, *Vanilla* Rosa Abreu-Runkel, *Vodka* Patricia Herlihy, *Water* Ian Miller,
Whiskey Kevin R. Kosar, *Wine* Marc Millon, *Yoghurt* June Hersh

Pie

A Global History

Janet Clarkson

REAKTION BOOKS

Published by Reaktion Books Ltd
Unit 32, Waterside
44–48 Wharf Road
London N1 7UX, UK
www.reaktionbooks.co.uk

First published 2009, reprinted 2022

Printed and bound in India by Replika Press Pvt. Ltd

British Library Cataloguing in Publication Data

Clarkson, Janet
Pie : a global history. – (Edible)
1. Pie
I. Title
641.8'24

ISBN 978 1 86189 425 0

Contents

Prologue: Preliminary Observations on Pie

> I may not be able to define a pie, but I know one when I see it.
> *Raymond Sokolov*

It behoves, I am told, every author to consider the scope of her work before launching into it. No problem, I thought. It is simple. It is about Pie. It is also, I am told, essential for the author to describe the scope of her work at its beginning, in order to forewarn her readers. Simple, I thought. I will start by defining Pie. In the end, I failed utterly. I would have agonized less over my failure had I remembered the above quotation rather earlier in the piece than I did. If the illustrious and erudite Raymond Sokolov cannot define pie, who am I even to attempt it? Nevertheless, I don't regret the attempt, as it was fascinating and enlightening in ways that I would not have suspected.

I began with a memory I had of a venison pie I once ordered at an upmarket restaurant. After exactly the right anticipatory interval my dinner arrived. It was very elegant. On a base of fluffy garlic mashed potatoes was a cleverly layered construction of julienned vegetables topped with slivers of tender, rare venison, the whole surmounted with a precariously balanced disc of puff pastry. It was delicious, but it was not pie. I was quite sure that it was not pie. Clearly, the chef and I had vastly differing opinions on the issue, which brought me to an early epiphany. When – and if – I came up with my concise, accurate definition of pie, not everyone else in the world would agree with it.

But surely there would be some areas of consensus as a starting point? Pies are not pies simply because they are called pies. The American treat called Eskimo pie, for example, is unequivocally ice cream, and moon pie is a chocolate biscuit with pretensions. Boston cream pie is certainly a cake, but apparently called pie because it is baked in a pie tin, by which logic I could cook porridge in a pie pan and call it 'porridge pie'. Other 'pies' are more problematic. Is a sausage roll a small pie? Should I include cobbler and pandowdy, which seem like failed pies with broken lids? Traditional Scottish black bun and English simnel cake are fruit cakes with pastry shells. Do they count? I pondered cottage pie and shepherd's pie. These have a layered pie-like structure certainly, but were (to me) instantly definable as not 'real' pies. Why not? Another epiphany dawned. Because they have no pastry. It seemed that my attempt at definition was devolving into a set of minimal criteria, at least for the purposes of this book. This second epiphany led to the First Law of Pies: 'No Pastry, No Pie'.

For reasons which will become apparent in chapter One, I immediately came up with the Second Law of Pies: they must be baked, not fried (or boiled, or steamed). One more law as to the number and location of crusts required (single top, single bottom, or double), and my criteria would be set – or so I thought. Formulating the Third Law of Pies proved to be an extraordinarily difficult part of the challenge, and I am still far from sure that I have resolved it in a satisfactory manner. I began my crust count with the *Oxford English Dictionary*, which asserts that a pie is:

Pie shapes,
from *The Queen's
Royal Cookery* by
T. Hall, 1713.

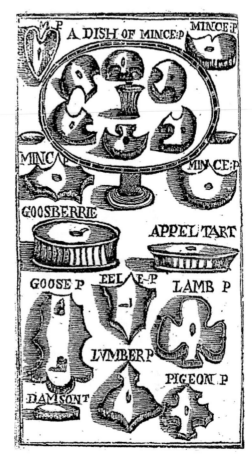

A baked dish of fruit, meat, fish or vegetables, covered
with pastry (or a similar substance) and freq. also having
a base and sides of pastry. Also (chiefly *N. Amer.*): a baked
open pastry case filled with fruit; a tart or flan.

It would seem then, that the editors of the *Oxford
English Dictionary* are of the opinion that, to qualify as a pie,

the top crust is essential and the bottom crust optional, except in America where it is the bottom crust that has primacy. They also appear to be suggesting that the bottom-crust American pie is, according to British-English usage, a tart or flan. The definition becomes less clear when they go on to describe a flan as 'an open tart', and a tart as 'the same, or nearly the same as a pie'.

I, who love and revere the *Oxford English Dictionary*, have to admit that it displays a lack of clarity in respect of pies and tarts, as indeed does most of the English-speaking world. Nowhere has this been more passionately demonstrated than in an extraordinary debate in the correspondence pages of *The Times* in 1927. In September of that year, a Mr R. A. Walker was moved to write a letter of 'vigorous protest' on 'the abominable soul-slaughtering and horrible trick of serving puff pastry and stewed fruit under the guise of apple tart', for which he blamed restaurateurs. Mr Walker's issue was to do with pie quality, but he was quickly taken to task by Colonel John C. Somerville for using 'apple pie' and 'apple tart' as alternatives. The Colonel could not 'for one moment allow' this, remarking that 'all properly brought up children' would know the difference. He went on to define 'pie' as 'whatever is cooked in a pie dish under a pastry roof', whereas 'when the fruit lies exposed in a flat substratum of pastry, then, and only then, can it be rightly called a tart'. A surprisingly passionate debate ensued over the next two weeks, with veiled insults and categorical statements being made and side issues being thrown in. Several expatriate American and French readers weighed in with their opinions and, as the discussion was becoming rather heated, 'an advocate of concise nomenclature' appeared in the form of Professor Henry E. Armstrong. The professor 'heartily supported' the discussion, and proceeded to give, as his best example, 'rice pie,

Abraham Bosse, 'La Boutique du pâtissier'. Note the pie moulds hanging from hooks.

always with an emphasis on pie'. He described 'rice, with a due amount of sugar and a plentitude of farmhouse milk' baked 'in a pie-dish; therefore a pie, the more because – in the jargon of the scientific – it is delicately auto-encrusted'. He clarified that this dish was not pudding, because 'a pudding must be boiled in a cloth and have a crust, but without sign of brown'. The professor's academic field was not indicated, but his slightly pompous opinion precipitated an indignant response from Mr E. E. Newton, who called his expertise into question, declaring that 'he cannot be a professor of cookery'. Mr Newton pointed out that the 'crust' of the professor's pie was simply the skin formed by the heat of the oven, whereas a pie has a 'crust formed of something different from the contents'. Another offended correspondent asked 'the stickler' how he would classify the famous Kentish 'pudding-pie' with its 'substratum and deep vertical wall of pastry . . . filled to the brim with custard and cooked in a container in an oven' and warned: 'If you want this dish in Kent, don't ask for custard tart.'

The Times staff ran a short editorial in the middle of all of this hearty support and indignant rebuttal, for the sake of 'all who hold that a pie is not a tart and a tart is not a pie'. The article acknowledged that the 'great Oxford Dictionary' and Mr Fowler's book on modern English usage 'throw up the sponge' in the matter of pie and tart, and it also gently chided Professor Armstrong for bringing puddings into the debate in an unhelpful manner. The discussion was to receive some 'authoritative support' in the form of an opinion from the manager of that bastion of English cuisine, Simpson's on the Strand. Mr F. W. Heck was unexpectedly humble. He did not want to add unduly to the correspondence, making 'a suggestion, or rather a plea, that English people should do their best to combat the tendency there seems to be these days to re-dress old English words with new meanings'. He invoked Charles Dickens, saying that that gentleman would have had no doubt what he meant by pie, and he would have meant, and got, 'that delicacy, made in a pie-dish, the interior having been cooked together with and under its golden pastry cover'.

Another authority in the unlikely form of Mr Gladstone was quoted a week later by Mrs Hugh Wyndham, who had heard him 'declaim on the subject with fervour and elegance'. He apparently contended that 'pie should be used only for fruit, that for meat, pasty was the right word'. It might have been expected that this would open up a whole new discussion on the pie/pasty issue but perhaps *The Times* readers were getting bored with the topic, for there were no responses. A final letter came from Mr Frank Birdwood, who stated with

Making a prune tart, late 19th century.

great confidence that the words 'tart' and 'torture' spring from the same Latin root and that 'it is certainly the case that the tart gets its name from the twisted (i.e. tortured) lengths of pastry with which the jam, or other principal ingredient, is still usually decorated, leaving it in all other respects "open".'

The 'gay battle of the tarts and pies' was formally ended on 12 October by an editorial piece announcing the commencement of the official 'pudding season'. The editors seemed relieved to note the copious consumption of puddings (sweet and savoury) by the English, this apparently indicating that: 'At the heart of the Empire, at any rate, our ancient stamina is not altogether lost.'

The professor who extolled the virtues of rice pie in *The Times'* debate could have found support for his argument in a decision made by the Supreme Court of America in 1910 that rice pudding was pastry. It all began when John Mylonopoulos rented the front part of a store to John Cobatos, one of the conditions being that the latter would not sell several specific items including 'pastry of any sort'. Some time later, Mr Cobatos commenced selling both prunes and rice pudding, managing close to 3,000 plates of the pudding in the next 47 days. Mr Mylonopoulos sued. The first judge crossed prunes off the claim immediately, dropping them 'into the respectable obscurity which is their humble but happy history'. The rice pudding issue was sent to a jury, which decided that it was pastry. Naturally there was an appeal. In spite of Mr Cobatos's counsel's 'fiery oration', quotations from many dictionaries and discussion of common understanding of the nature of rice pudding, the appeal was lost. Plaintiff Mylonopoulos was awarded his $101.05 damages and $21.50 costs.

If the *Oxford English Dictionary*, the erudite nineteenth-century readers of *The Times* and the Supreme Court of the United States fail to reach consensus on the question, 'What, exactly, is a pie?', then for the purposes of this book, I feel free to make up my own rules on the crust issue. Historically, one of the seminal features of a pie is its ability to be eaten out of the hand, so this would seem to exclude pot-pies. I leaned towards this restriction for a while, but common sense and common usage prevailed, and the proposed Third Law became redundant: any number of crusts would qualify, but these must (as stated in the First Law) be of pastry. Pastry, not a 'similar substance' – a decision based, I believe, on sound historic reasons which will be revealed in chapter One.

Words often give clues to the origin of things, and I hoped to learn much about the history of the pie from the word 'pie'. The *Oxford English Dictionary* gives its first known use as being in the expense accounts of the Bolton Priory in Yorkshire in 1303 (although the surname 'Pyman' is recorded in 1301), but admits that its origin is uncertain and that 'no further related word is known outside English'. It suggests that the word is identical in form to the same word meaning 'magpie' which 'is held by many to have been in some way derived from or connected with that word'. The suggested connection is that a pie has contents of a 'miscellaneous nature', similar to the magpie's colouring or to the odds and ends picked up and used by the bird to adorn its nest. As support for the argument the *Oxford English Dictionary* notes the similarity between the words haggis (the Scots dish with contents of a miscellaneous nature) and an old French word for magpie (*agace or agasse*).

The only other possible origin mooted by the *Oxford English Dictionary* is that the word 'pie' – meaning a baked pastry – may be connected with the same word used in an agricultural context for 'a collection of things made into a heap', such as potatoes or other produce covered with earth and straw for storage. But perhaps there is another clue buried in the *Oxford English Dictionary*. The Gaelic word *pige* (or one of its variants) may be related to the English dialect word *piggin*, which can mean a wooden pail, or an earthen pot such as might be used for cooking. If a non-linguist may be permitted an idea, could there be a connection here? The early history of the pie, which will be explored in chapter One, would suggest that this is possible, and it is surely no less tenuous a connection than that with a bird?

A French linguistic connection cannot be dismissed completely either. The English language was never the same again after the Normans invaded in 1066, and a whole lot of pie-words are similar enough in French and English to suggest a

A Victorian engraving of a child attacking a pie with great vigour.

similar origin – think tart and *tourte,* for example. We will come across a few others in later chapters, but the most intriguing are the words paste, pastry and pasta, which are all variations on a theme of flour and water, and have a common origin. The French word pâté comes from the same root, which is more obvious when you discover that the circumflex over the 'a' replaces a missing 's', indicating that a pâté used to have a pastry crust. Modern pâté is pastry-less, so the original form now has to be qualified as a pâté *en croûte (croûte* meaning 'crust'). The most fascinating connection is that 'pasty' also appears to come from this same root, raising the question of why this specific type of pastry-wrapped food got a name with a totally different origin to that of the ordinary 'pie'.

I

A Brief History of Pie

Pyes were but indigested lumps of dough,
'Till time and just expence improv'd them so.
Of Apple-Pyes; A poem, by Mr Welsted (1750)

Once upon a time, *everything* baked in an oven that was not bread was 'pie'. *Everything.* Let me explain.

It seems likely that the earliest ovens were actually kilns, used to fire clay objects such as figurines and pots. Bread, meanwhile, was baked in flat cakes on hot hearthstones. Someone, somewhere, perhaps, noted the similarity between clay and dough and, in an act born either of inspired impulse or thoughtful experimentation, tossed the dough into the kiln instead. The bread oven was born. Meat, meanwhile, was cooked by direct exposure to the fire, on a spit or in the coals. The problem with cooking meat this way is that even if it does not burn, the valuable and tasty juices drip away and the meat dries and shrinks. Other cooks at other times got around this problem by wrapping the meat up to protect it – in leaves, for example. Or clay. Clay that, to another cook in perhaps another time and place, felt just like dough. This last inspired step created the primitive meat pie – something medieval cooks called a 'bake-mete'.

A French baker's shop, from the *Kalendrier des Bergères*, about 1499.

The thick crust of this early pie acted like a baking dish. For hundreds of years it was the only form of baking container – meaning *everything* was pie. The crust also, as it turned out, performed two other useful functions: it acted as a carrying and storage container (before lunch boxes) and, by virtue of excluding air, as a method of preservation (before canning and refrigeration). These early piecrusts were called 'coffins', which sounds vaguely sinister today, as if our ancestors were already implying that the contents of a pie could be doubtful. In actual fact the word originally meant a basket or box (think of a *coffret* of perfume), and was used in relation to pastry 'caskets' before it came to refer to the funeral variety.

But what was this crust actually like to eat? We know that it was often made several inches thick to withstand many hours of baking, so it would have been very hard. It is usually referred to in modern texts as inedible, and *not meant to be eaten*. As a blanket statement I find this hard to believe. Certainly to our delicate modern sensibilities, it sounds unpalatable – but we are talking about harder times, when growing and harvesting grain and producing flour – even very coarse flour – was an incredibly labour-intensive process. It is surely not likely that such a hard-won resource was simply discarded after the contents were eaten, even in the great houses? The crust may not have been intended for lords and ladies, but the well-to-do were obliged to feed their servants and were also expected to feed the local poor. Would not this largesse of sauce-soaked crust be distributed to the scullery boys and the hungry clamouring at the gate?

There are suggestions in early manuscripts that the crusts were, at least occasionally, reused. One fifteenth-century manuscript for 'Fresh Lamprey Bakyn' (a lamprey pie) suggests that, after the lamprey is eaten, the remaining juice may be boiled up with wine, sugar and spices and then poured

A fifteenth-century French banquet, from *Roman de Lancelot en prose* by Jean Fouquet.

back into the coffin, which has been refilled with layers of 'white brede', creating a new dish called 'soppys in galentyn'. Sometimes the baked dough was recycled as a thickening agent, such as in one seventeenth-century recipe for a 'Spanish Olio' which suggests that 'some Crusts of Bread, or Venison Pye-Crust' be added before the stew is boiled 'in all five or six hours gently'. In other words, it was used as we would use a *roux*.

Thankfully, the problem of what to do with excruciatingly hard leftover baked dough eventually went away, as we will see.

The Invention of Pastry

After a few millennia of inspiration, the primitive clay oven gave rise to the gleaming modern steel version. A high-tech oven alone does not, however, turn a bake-mete into a pie as we know it. One more important development was necessary. Pastry had to be invented.

Dough becomes pastry when fat is added. Not just any dough, not just any fat, and not just by any random method of mixing. Exactly when and where and how this happened are mysteries that we will never completely solve as it all took place long before our earliest surviving cookbooks were written. We can make some educated guesses, however, and some of our clues come from considering the crucial difference between 'dough' and 'pastry'. For this we need to make a brief foray into food chemistry.

The key is gluten. Gluten is a protein with long, elastic molecules which simultaneously enable the dough to be made stronger (by providing structure) and lighter (by enabling the trapping of air bubbles). A lot of gluten means a firm

Apple pie, from *The Modern Housewife* by Alexis Soyer.

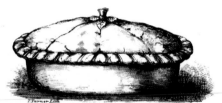

PHYSIOLOGY OF TARTS, PIES, AND PIE CRUST.

PORTRAIT OF AN APPLE PIE
AS IT OUGHT TO BE
TAKEN FROM STILL LIFE.

STRIKING LIKENESS OF AN APPLE TART IN A PIE
AS THEY OFTEN ARE
TAKEN FROM REAL LIFE.

Made with the same materials, at the same cost, baked at the same baker's, at the same time, in the same oven, but executed by two different feminine artistes. We regret that neither portrait is signed.

Having seen both Pies made at two different houses, but by the same receipt, I sent my servant to watch the process of the baking of them; after waiting till they were done, she informed me, that about one o'clock a very cleanly dressed little girl presented herself at the baker's, with a ticket bearing the name of "Mrs. Armstrong;" No. 1 Pie was then delivered to her.

"A few minutes after," says she, "a tall untidy looking girl, with a black face and still blacker hands, with her hair floating *à la tempesta,* called for Mrs. Jenkims's Apple Tart; No. 2 was handed to her, she exclaiming very loudly as she took it up, 'O Lor! aint it nice and smoking hot.'

"In the crowd," says my Mary, "I lost sight of both tarts."

structure, which is ideal for bread, but bad for pastry. Too little gluten means no structure and no air-trapping, so flat bread and tough pastry. The task of the pastry-cook is to get just the right amount of gluten to make the pastry light and crumbly and flaky. How is this done?

Wheat is the only grain with a significant amount of gluten, so we have our first clue to the origins of pastry. Superb pastry could only have developed where wheat was

grown: rye, barley and oats do not make good pastry, nor
do rice or maize or potato starch. The gluten content of the
final wheat dough can be manipulated by the cook in a
number of ways depending on the ultimate goal, whether it
be sturdy bread or flaky pastry. These tricks of the pastry-
cook's trade give us further clues to the development of
pastry itself.

The first trick is to use exactly the right amount of water, for it is water that activates the gluten in flour. Fat is the second trick, and it helps the texture of pastry in a number of ways. Fat coats little packets of flour, waterproofing them and limiting the amount of water that gets in (less water, so less gluten), and it keeps the gluten strands 'short' and slippery. Little smears and gobbets of fat also physically separate the mini layers of dough, so that they form individual flakes or crumbs, not a solid mass. It goes without saying, then, that the proportion of fat to flour used is crucial in controlling the final texture of the pastry, but it is not the only factor.

Like flours, not all fats are created equal. Oil is fat that is liquid at room temperature – there is no other essential difference – but good pastry cannot be made with oil. Flour simply absorbs the oil and the resulting dough is mealy, not tender and flaky. The ideal fat for pastry-making is one with a high melting point because the longer it takes for the fat to melt, the longer it keeps the little parcels of dough separate, generating little packets of steam to puff and lighten the dough. Pig fat (lard) has a high melting point and very little water content, so is ideal on both counts. Butter melts at body temperature so does not give quite such a good texture, but the trade-off is a richer flavour. So now we have our second clue to the whereabouts of pastry development: truly delicious, light, 'short' pastry could only develop where there was a good supply of solid fat, which in essence means where there are pigs or cows.

Pastry-making, as every amateur baker fears, is as much about technique as ingredients. The rationale behind the well-known advice to keep the hands, implements and kitchen cool while making pastry, to use minimal water and to handle it lightly is obvious, now that we understand the process.

Cool handling lengthens the time that the fat in the dough stays solid; using the minimum amount of water reduces the gluten content and also allows the dough to be crisper; minimal handling also reduces the gluten, so we do not knead pastry dough as we do bread.

As far as a time-frame for these developments goes, we can probably reasonably deduce that the pie began its life some time before the fourteenth century in those areas of Europe where wheat was grown and pigs and cattle reared. There does not seem to be any doubt that a huge variety of pies was made in northern and central Europe throughout the Middle Ages, and this was also partly because the forests of northern Europe provided an abundance of fuel (and fodder for pigs) long after those of the south had been depleted. Why is this important? Because the grand bakemetes and pies (which might contain a whole haunch of venison) took a long time to bake and required a lot of fuel.

Size is not the only thing that matters in pies of course. Another branch of the pastry art resulted in the elegant tarts and small pastries – particularly the sweet ones – that most of us find irresistible. It seems likely that the basic idea of small sweet pastries came to Europe from the Arab world during the expansion of the Muslim empire in the seventh

Italian fresco, 15th century, showing a baker putting pies in an oven with a long 'peel'.

Vincenzo Campi, *The Kitchen*, 1580s, oil on canvas.

century, but it is probable that it was the northern Italians of the Renaissance who refined and developed pastry into the many glorious incarnations we appreciate today. All of the resources were in place, and the context was right. Wheat from northern Italy is 'soft' – that is, it is already low in gluten so is ideal for pastry-making. Butter was the fat of choice for cooking in northern Italy (and a sign of wealth), compared with the oil of the south of the country, and there is no doubt that butter makes the finest pastry for sweet pies and tarts. The philosophical environment of the Renaissance encouraged the development of all the arts, and the dynastic families of Italy had no shortage of money for indulging their lust for the good things of life. Brilliant and innovative cooks were coveted and encouraged, and there was a grand blossoming of culinary ideas and techniques which gradually spread to France and the rest of Europe.

The situation in Britain was different. In Britain, butter was food for the poor. The wealthy in Britain preferred lard,

Woodcut from the late 15th-century *Le Grant Calendrier et Compost des Bergiers.*
It was common in medieval times for feasts to include nude bathing. Here, a
raised pie awaits the couple finishing their frolic in the bath.

maybe because the animal had to be killed to obtain the
fat, thus its perceived value was higher. Lard makes superb
huge 'raised' or 'standing' pies full of meat, which flour-
ished to become one of the jewels in England's culinary
crown.

The argument about whether or not medieval pastry
was meant to be eaten is a relative one. What we really want
to know is how much of it was designed to be eaten as an
intrinsic and desirable part of the dish. There are sugges-

tions in the earliest cookbooks that at least some of the time this was certainly the case. Why else would a cookbook writer specify that the pastry be made thin and 'tender as ye maye'? This instruction appears in the first-known written recipe for pastry, in a little book called *A Propre New Booke of Cokery*, published in London in 1545:

To make short paest for tarte

Take fyne floure and a cursey of fayre water and a dyshe of swete butter and a lyttel saffron, and the yolckes of two egges and make it thynne and tender as ye maye.

The instructions in early cookbooks are, for a food historian, frustratingly lacking in detail as they were based on much assumed knowledge, and were intended as *aides-memoires* for experienced cooks. It is clear, however, that by the sixteenth century short, puff and perhaps choux pastries were already established, and there are tantalizing clues that they may have already been around for a couple of hundred years. The earliest-known cookbook from England, *The Forme Of Cury*, was compiled in about 1390 by the master-cooks of King Richard II, and it contains instructions for 'payn puff', which sounds suspiciously like puff pastry.

There is one particular type of pastry that has played an important role in the history of the pie and that breaks a few of the method rules. It spans the bridge between bread dough and regular pastry, and can still be found in the traditional English pork pie such as that made famous in Melton Mowbray in Leicestershire. It is what we refer to now as 'hot water pastry'. Its great advantage over bread dough and other types of pastry is that it can be sculpted like clay, allowing it to be 'raised' to form free-standing crusts. A whole lot more possibilities opened up when raised crusts

A genuine Melton Mowbray pie.

were developed, as they allowed 'wet' fillings such as stews, fruits and custards to be cooked in them.

Before baking dishes, then, dough in one form or another was used as the 'container' – so by definition everything cooked in an oven was 'pie'. The legacy of this persists in a number of food words that don't at first glance seem to have anything to do with pie. 'Custard' comes from *croustade* or crust, which the *Oxford English Dictionary* defines as 'formerly, a kind of open pie containing pieces of meat or fruit covered with a preparation of broth or milk, thickened with eggs, sweetened, and seasoned with spices, etc.'. A 'dariole' is now a small mould for baking soft puddings or creams, but once it meant a small pie 'filled with flesh, hearbes, and spices, mingled and minced together'. Even a 'rissole' was once 'a sort of minced pie' that was usually fried (from the French *rissoler*, to fry brown).

These adapted pie-words are the lucky ones – many more have completely disappeared. When was the last time you saw on a menu a *chewet* (a small round pie of finely chopped meat or fish, with spices and fruit, 'made taller than a marrow pie'), a *dowlet* (a small pie of particularly dainty little tidbits), a *herbelade* or *hebolace* (a pie with a pork mince and herb mixture), a *talemouse* (a sort of cheesecake, sometimes triangular in shape) or a *vaunt* (a type of fruit pie)? These words (and more) were once everyday words in a baker's vocabulary. The only conclusion it is possible to draw is that the loss of so many pie-words reflects the loss of the pies themselves.

Is the Pie Dead?

The importance of the pie – once the 'meat and potatoes' of the English – began to slip with the increased cultivation of the actual potato in the nineteenth century. As the nineteenth became the twentieth century, social changes pushed the pie further into decline. The 'great pies' had their last glorious days in the English manor houses of the Edwardian era, before the domestic classes left to fight the First World War. The ordinary family dinner pie hung onto its place a little longer – it was alive and well during the Second World War – until the housewife increasingly became a working wife with less time for cooking. Since then, our sense of being time-poor has escalated enormously. Naturally, we gave up the most time-consuming and intimidating cooking first. Simultaneously, we have been subjected to the overwhelming propaganda of the nutrition police. Whichever way you look at it, the homemade pie has been under siege for a century at least, and surely its survival is endangered.

The strangely marvellous thing is that, we refuse to relinquish the pie. We cling to the *idea* of it with some fervour, in spite of its fading reality on our tables. Why is it so? What is it *about* pies?

2

The Universal Appeal of Pie

A boy doesn't have to go to war to be a hero; he can say he
doesn't like pie when he sees there isn't enough to go around.

Edgar Watson Howe

There was no doubt in the minds of nineteenth-century
cooks and cookbook writers that there was *something* about
pie – a difficult to grasp something that made it universally
esteemed in a way that cake or stew or soup was not. A few
quotations will suffice to demonstrate.

In 1806, Mrs Rundell began her 'Observations on Savoury
Pies' in her bestseller, *A New System of Domestic Cookery*, with
the confident statement: 'There are few articles of cookery
more generally liked than relishing pies, if properly made.'
The celebrated chef Alexis Soyer noted the everyday importance of pies in the Victorian era in his *Shilling Cookery for the
People* (1860):

> From childhood we eat pies – from girlhood to boyhood
> we eat pies – from middle age to old age we eat pies – in
> fact, pies in England may be considered as one of our
> best companions *du voyage* through life. It is we who leave
> them behind, not they who leave us; for our children

Child wearing a bakers' hat and apron while eating a pie.

and grandchildren will be as fond of pies as we have been; therefore it is needful that we should learn how to make them, and make them well! Believe me, I am not jesting, but if all the spoilt pies made in London on one single Sunday were to be exhibited in a row beside a railway line, it would take above an hour by special train to pass in review these culinary victims.

The pie was placed on an even higher pedestal by the social journalist, Charles Manby Smith in his book *Curiosities of London Life* (1853), where he declared it 'a great human discovery which has universal estimation among all civilized eaters'.

There will always be naysayers of course, but the few dyspeptic curmudgeons and ascetics who disagree on the appeal of the pie only serve to prove the rule. Ambrose Bierce in his *Devil's Dictionary* was perhaps merely demonstrating his need for medical advice when he defined the pie as 'an advance agent of the reaper whose name is Indigestion'. The nineteenth-century nutrition guru Sylvester Graham managed to convince a significant percentage of the American public that the answer to all of society's

Medieval picnic.

Detail from Claude Monet, *Déjeuner sur l'herbe,* 1865–6.

problems and the guarantee of heavenly reward was a strict regime of cold baths, bland food and sexual restraint, and that cholera was caused by chicken pies. Had he lived a few decades longer and seen the evidence that cholera was due to contaminated water, poor Graham may have allowed himself an occasional pie to compensate for all that sexual restraint.

The Usefulness of Pie

The original pie served three very useful functions in acting as a baking, carrying and preserving container. We now have more efficient ways to perform these functions, but the pie is still an extraordinarily pragmatic food for both cooks and consumers. For sheer versatility the pie is impossible to beat. It is useful in ways that bread (very useful) and soup (somewhat useful) are not, precisely because of this versatility. Pies can be eaten hot or cold, at every course of every meal from breakfast to supper, not forgetting at picnics and while travelling, and they are especially suited to meal-in-the-hand events. They can be economical or extravagant, an everyday meal or a special feast, a simple food or a powerful symbol. The fillings can be as varied as circumstances, imagination and conscience will allow, and the crust is a superb opportunity to show off the artistic as well as the culinary skill of the cook.

An outstanding historical feature of the pie is that it is a self-contained meal which can be eaten in the hand, without need of cutlery, crockery or napery. This ultra-convenient aspect of the pie might be one reason for its success in England. Sheila Hutchins, in her book *English Recipes* (1967), says: 'The sporting English aristocrats with their passionate

A medieval portable pie oven.

Poster from the United War Work Campaign, First World War.

interest in cock-fighting or cricket had early developed a system for eating well without interfering with whatever might be on hand.' Hutchins illustrates this with the story of the Earl of Sandwich, reluctant to leave the gaming tables one night in 1762 and calling for a piece of beef between two slices of bread, immortalizing his name in the process. It is an amusing myth which I do not understand. The era and the country were famous for pies. Why would he not have called for a bit of pie left over from dinner?

The reheatability of pies can be both an advantage (usually to the cook) and a disadvantage (usually to the consumer). Chaucer knew this well in the fourteenth century, and illustrated it beautifully in his *Canterbury Tales*. The Cook is challenged to tell his own story to make up for serving reheated pies (from which he had already siphoned off some of the gravy) to the pilgrims:

> Now telle on, Roger; looke that it be good,
>   For many a pastee hastow laten blood,
> And many a Jakke of Dovere hastow soold
> That hath been twies hoot and twies coold

A 'Jack of Dover' was a bottle of wine made up of collected dregs from other bottles, recorked and sold as new. Chaucer uses this as a metaphor for the repeatedly reheated pies, making the idea even more distasteful by describing the Cook as a dirty man with suppurating sores on his legs.

When Soyer said of pies that they are 'one of our best companions *du voyage* through life', he was referring to consumers, but he might just as well have been referring to his professional colleagues, for pies have always been enormously useful to caterers and cooks, particularly at events where a large number must be fed efficiently. In modern times this is usually at sporting events such as football games, but the original experts in mass catering were the military. On 11 July 1891 the visiting German emperor reviewed the troops at Wimbledon. The Post Office Volunteers had Quartermaster Dickson in charge, and he invented an efficient, spectacularly simple system which impressed the journalist who described it:

> Each man as he passed took without halting a tankard in one hand and received a pork pie in the other, then passing on to enjoy his luncheon a hundred yards off. The result was that about 800 men were served in exactly seven and a half minutes.

Quartermaster Dickson was way ahead of his time. Eight hundred customers in seven and a half minutes would be an amazing achievement for the fastest modern fast-food outlet.

Biology Makes Us Do It

There is no escaping a biological fact that is the despair of dieters everywhere. For survival reasons we are genetically programmed to crave nutrient-dense foods (such as pies), eat as much as possible of them while they are available and convert them efficiently into body fat in readiness for the next famine. Primitive humans did not need to develop a craving for fibre and antioxidants: life was already nasty, brutish and far too short for these to add any value. So, how did early *Homo sapiens* determine what foods are nutrient-dense without the help of nutritionists and dieticians?

We are attracted first, by smell. Our noses detect the volatile components in our chemical environment, and these are increased by heating. We should expect then that the smell of cooked high-fat, high-protein foods would be the most appealing to us as a species, and it appears that this is indeed the case. At a simple biological level, before dieticians were invented, our noses decided what was best to eat: if it smelled good, it was almost certainly good to eat. When VAT (British goods and services tax) legislation was first being formulated in the UK, bakers successfully argued that hot meat pies should be VAT-free as the major reason for having them hot on the premises was to create an enticing smell, rather than to provide a special service – and even the most uninspired pie smells enticing while it is hot.

For a long time in the West it was believed that our taste buds could only determine four basic flavours – sweet, salty, sour and bitter. Most scientists now accept what the Japanese have known for hundreds of years, that there is a fifth taste called *umami*. This is a concept of 'delicious flavour' or 'savouriness' such as that we taste in aged cheeses, roasted meat and Asian fish sauce. The taste is conveyed primarily by glutamates, which are amino acids, which in turn are the building blocks of protein. It makes sense, biologically, that we would have built-in protein detectors. Sweet foods are a source of calories, salt foods help us keep our chemistry in balance, sour and bitter tastes make us wary as in nature they often signify a poison. *Umami* wakes up our protein sensors. Mother's milk has *umami* (ten times the glutamates of cows' milk). Meat pies have *umami* too.

There is also a third process going on when we eat: the tactile appreciation of the food, the sense of its 'body' or richness – that sensation we call 'mouthfeel'. If our enjoyment of food were simply about taste and smell (and perhaps, now that we are civilized, appearance) we could purée a pie, put it in a glass and decorate it with a paper umbrella and still enjoy it. A pie is only as good as its pastry, and one of the delights of a good pie is the contrast in texture between the crisp pastry and the filling – whatever it might be. In a perfect pie, each component is independently perfect – the mouthfeel of the pastry (buttery, flaky, crumbly) and the mouthfeel of the filling (rich, unctuous, tender, sticky, crunchy etc.); and the whole is more than the sum of its parts.

So is the pie not the perfect food for the senses? Does any other single dish have such potential?

Beyond Calories

It seems that the *liking* of pies has a sound biological base, but nutrient density alone is not sufficient for modern humans, or we would eat whale blubber with the same relish that we eat pie. We are social animals, and we don't usually find and eat food alone, so we associate it at an emotional level with people, events and circumstances. Eventually a food becomes embedded with meaning, allowing anthropologists to ask questions like: 'Do pies *mean* anything?'

Smell can be a powerful trigger of emotion because humans make associations between smells and the social

Arthur Hughes, *The Skipper and his Crew (Saying Grace)*, 1881, oil on canvas.

and emotional context in which they are perceived. Some intriguing work has been done on 'olfactory evoked recall' at the Smell and Taste Treatment and Research Foundation in Chicago. Of course, the subjects were all from the Chicago area, and likely had European ancestors (as does pie), so the results may not apply to other demographics. Nevertheless, the results are interesting. The smells giving rise to the most nostalgia were from baked foods (bread, cakes etc.), closely followed by those from cooked meat dishes such as bacon or meatballs and spaghetti. It sounds to me that if there had been a separate meat pie category it would have combined the associations of both and won hands down.

This is nothing new to many non-scientists of course. Estate agents have long known it, which is why they advise vendors to have a pot of freshly brewed coffee in the house to make it smell like a home when potential buyers visit. Proust explained it better than anyone before or since when he described the flood of memories triggered by the scent of a buttery little cake dipped in fragrant lime-blossom tea.

Craig Claiborne said: 'I have learned that nothing can equal the universal appeal of the food of one's childhood and early youth.' It is the food that looks backwards through our shared family memories. It is comfort food, the food inextricably linked in our cultural consciousness with motherhood and nationhood. Even though pies are no longer a daily item on our dinner tables, they still figure large in many of our memories: pies mean Thanksgiving and Christmas and picnics and silly old Aunt Mabel and going to the football with Dad. The pie-cook and the pie-consumer are both lucky if the smell of the pie 'sells' not only its desirability as biological fuel but also the remembrance of pies past.

There is one other meaning of pie, particularly the homemade one, which sums up its universal esteem. In the words of Margaret Fulton, 'A pie is invariably acclaimed as a treat and a sign of a caring cook.' A cook who has gone to extra trouble, who loves you enough not just to toss the stew onto a plate with a lump of bread, but to craft for it its own little pastry gift-box. Is this the crux of it?

3
Pies by Design

The fine arts are five in number, namely: painting, sculpture,
poetry, music, and architecture, the principal branch of the latter
being pastry.

Antonin Carême (Marie-Antoine Carême)

It is ironic that Antonin Carême (1784–1833), a man revered
as 'the chef of kings and king of chefs', had he had a choice,
would probably have studied architecture. His culinary
career came about by default when, as a child abandoned by
destitute parents, he found work as a lowly kitchen boy. He
spent the rest of his working life in the kitchen, but at heart
he remained an architect, expressing his passion through the
design and construction of the incredibly ornate *pièces mon-
tées* which were his signature.

Maybe Carême had a point. A pie, like a building,
requires construction after all. Also like a building, one size
and style of pie does not fit all fillings and occasions.
Architects of the early twentieth century may have thought
they invented the idea of 'form follows function', but pastry-cooks had been quietly applying the principle for hundreds of years. A pie containing a whole side of venison and
intended to preserve the meat for a prolonged period of

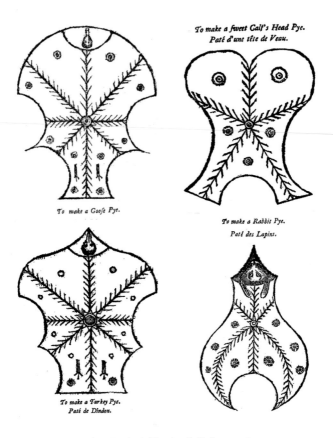

To make a sweet Calf's Head Pye.
Paté d'une tête de Veau.

To make a Goose Pye.

To make a Rabbit Pye.
Paté des Lapins.

To make a Turkey Pye.
Paté de Dindon.

Pie shapes from John Thacker's *The Art of Cookery*, 1758.

time is a design-world away from a delicate almond-milk custard acceptable for Lent, and a whole design-universe away from one containing the entirely non-culinary treat of a very alive, scantily clad young woman. Other circumstances dictate other designs: a pie might need to be robust enough to send on a long sea voyage, elegant enough to serve as a gift, clever enough to entertain, or awe-inspiring enough to deliver a message of power or propaganda.

43

Luckily for the housewife, as the seventeenth century progressed an increasing number of cookbooks were written for the non-professional, meaning that less knowledge was assumed. Luckily for us, they therefore give us more insight into the pastry and pie-making business. Gervase Markham in his *English Hus-wife* (1615) went to some pains to clarify the different sorts of pastry that were appropriate for different pies.

> Our English Hus-wife must be skilfull I pastery, and know how and in what manner to bake all sorts of meate, and what paste is fit for every meate, and how to handle and compound such pastes as for example, red Deere venison, wilde Boare, Gammons of Bacon, Swans, Elkes, Porpus, and such like standing dishes, which must be kept long, wold be bak't in a moyst, thicke rough course, and long lasting crust, and therefore of all other, your Rye-paste is best for that purpose: your Turkie, Capon, Pheasant, Partridge, Veale, Peacocks, Lambe, and all sorts of water-fowle, which are to come to the Table more then once (yet not many daies) would be bak't in a good white crust, somewhat thicke; therefore your Wheat is fit for them: your Chickens, Calves-feet, Olives, Potatoes, Quinces, Fallow Deere and such like, which are most commonly eaten hot, would be in the finest, shortest and thinnest crust; and therefore your fine wheate flower which is a little baked in the oven before it be kneaded is the best for that purpose.

Markham makes a point about pies 'which must be kept long' because this was one of their most important requirements in his day. Before refrigeration and canning were invented the only ways that meat could be preserved were by drying, smoking, salting – or encasing in a 'thicke rough course crust'. The pastry for pies 'to be kept long' was usually of rye flour, several inches thick, baked until very hard and 'not proposed for eating, but to keep the Inside properly'. When the pies were taken out of the oven, melted fat was poured in through a hole in the lid to exclude air, thus preserving the contents. Once the pie was cut this airtight seal was broken, leaving the contents prone to rapid spoilage – which perhaps gave rise to the old superstition that it is unlucky to take just one slice from a pie.

Some of the instructions in old cookbooks that don't make much sense to us today were perhaps intended to maximize the keeping potential of the pie. One fifteenth-century manuscript has an odd warning against getting saffron 'nygh the brinkes' (near the edges) of your pie, 'for then hit will never close'. As saffron was a common ingredient in both pastry and pie fillings at the time, this instruction is inexplicable. The instructions for joining pie-lid to base in the sixteenth-century German cookbook of Sabina Welserin start in a recognizable way for us with 'join it together well with the fingers', but then she advises:

> Leave a small hole. And see that it is pressed together well, so that it does not come open. Blow in the small hole which you have left, then the cover will lift itself up. Then quickly press the hole closed.

Was this just to make a nice domed top, or was it also to lift the dough off the wet contents? It was essential for the coffin crust to be kept very dry or it would lose its preserving power. In William Salmon's *Family-Dictionary, or, Houshold Companion* (1695) he gives a recipe for a boar pie sealed with butter that 'will, if it be not set in a very moist place, keep a

Wild boar pie.

whole Year'. Keeping a meat pie for a whole year without refrigeration is a terrifying thought today, but it was such a common practice that we have to assume that most of the time consumers survived the experience.

A thick dense crust also formed a robust container that enabled pies to be sent long distances over land and sea. There was a regular traffic in grand 'Yorkshire Christmas Pies' to London by rail in the nineteenth century, but this was nothing compared to some of the efforts made by devoted mothers and wives over the centuries in getting pies to their sons and husbands away at university or at war.

One worried mother was Lady Brilliana Harley of Brampton Bryan in Herefordshire. She regularly sent pies by carrier to her son Edward at university in Oxford in 1638–1639, a trip that would have taken several days by carrier. Ned survived his university days so it is to be assumed that her pies were robust and well sealed. On 10 May it was a kid pie:

I have made a pye to send to you; it is a kide pye. I beleeve you have not that meate ordinaryly at Oxford; one halfe is seasned with one kind of seasening, and the other with another.

Once the postal service was established, pies were sent by mail to destinations far and wide. The Post Office gave excellent advice in 1884 on how to do this at Christmas:

It is desirable that any Christmas presents – such, for instance, as contain holly, mistletoe, or other decorations, poultry, game, puddings, mince pies, or any other pastry, confectionary, apples, toys, fancy articles &c, – intended for transmission by parcel post should be carefully packed by the senders so as to preserve them from injury.

The very reliable Post Office even managed to avoid pilfering of the goodies en route. One English soldier in South Africa during the Boer War was moved to write to *The Times*:

I should like to say a word in praise of the postal and parcel arrangements out at the front . . . I am confident I have not missed a single parcel … in spite of the fact that I am continually imploring my people not to label parcels chocolate, game pie, chicken and tongue &c.

The Art of Pies

The architects who declared that 'form follows function' also declared that all ornamentation is bad. It is abundantly clear that pastry-cooks have never had any inclination to follow this philosophy. Pastry is an eminently artistic medium and generations of practitioners of the 'curious art of pastery' (curious as in its old meaning of 'ingenious, skilful, clever') have enthusiastically embraced its potential.

The technological advances of the Industrial Revolution enabled the manufacture of incredibly elaborate pie moulds, but well before that time pastry-cooks took advantage of the mouldability of hot-water crust to create pies 'made craftily in the lyknes of a byrde's bodye', or a castle, or a fish, or any other shape that that the baker's inner artist desired. Pies in the form of castles had an enduring popularity (perhaps all early pastry-cooks were frustrated architects?) There is a recipe in the *Forme of Cury* for a 'chastlete', which is a pastry castle with four crenellated towers around a central courtyard, each with a different filling and colour. At the end of the eighteenth century, Parson James Woodforde noted in his diary a meal which included 'beef-stake tarts in turretts of paste'.

Sometimes the lid of a large coffin was removed before serving, and replaced with a separately baked lid decorated to look like a heraldic shield, for example, or the lid was left off and the surface of the filling 'made as gay as you please' with herbs or flowers, or shapes cut from pastry or coloured jelly. One recipe from 1658 for a steak pie instructs that the lid be removed and fried sage leaves be stuck upright in the walls before serving, which must have made it look like a little indoor garden.

The seventeenth-century baker could call on paper templates 'cut into divers proportions, as Beasts, Birds, Arms, Knots, Flowers, and such like' to make pastry shapes which were often baked in advance, ready to decorate the tops of pies before serving. There were other parallels with needlework too: 'stump pies' were so called because they were

PATE-CHAUDS, OR RAISED PIES FOR ENTREES,

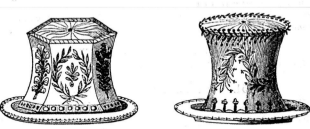

Pâté-Chaud Cases.

752. PATE-CHAUD* OF YOUNG RABBITS, WITH FINE-HERBS.

Highly decorated raised pies from *The Modern Cook* (1860), by Queen Victoria's chef Charles Elmé Francatelli.

embellished with such intricate pastry knots, flowers, heraldic symbols and so on that they resembled the three-dimensional form of embroidery popular in the Jacobean period known as 'stump work'.

Pastry artists of previous times also worked with colour: pie-lids might be frosted (with sugar mixed with rosewater), 'endored' ('gilded' with saffron, egg yolk or real gold), or painted with various colouring agents. Recipes for colouring agents appear in many books from the medieval period

49

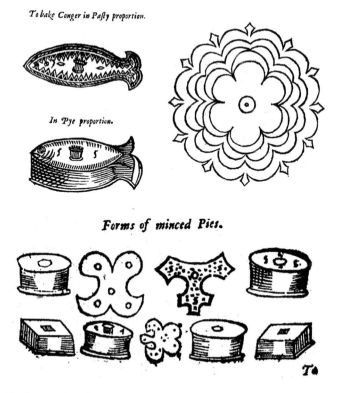

To bake Conger in Pasty proportion.

In Pye proportion.

Forms of minced Pies.

Pie shape outlines from *The Accomplish't Cook* (1660) by Robert May. The top-right diagram is for a Bride Pie (see pp. 82–4).

onwards, and some of them are very alarming. *The Widowes Treasure* (1586) gives a recipe for *An Emeraulde Greene* containing *verdegres* (copper acetate), *litarge* (lead oxide) and quicksilver (metallic mercury) mixed with 'the pisse of a young childe', and another for a gold colour containing saffron, *orpiment* (arsenic trisulphide) and the gall (bile) of a hare or a pike pounded together, placed in a vial, and buried in a dunghill for five days. It is perhaps better after all that some techniques have died out.

There was also an art to serving a pie properly in the days when they were often very large and were intended to feed many people. The elegant and correct carving of different joints of meat was an essential skill and an honoured role for a gentleman, who was also expected to know the correct terminology. He would, for example, 'dysmembre that heron, traunche that sturgyon, lyste that swanne, disfygure that pecocke' and 'border that pie'. He would also know that a pie should be opened at the top if it was to be served hot, and 'midways' if cold.

Naturally, if one is not to seem boorish, one should know how to eat a pie correctly. Thankfully, etiquette manuals have been around for centuries to show how this should be done. A book of manners published in 1609 and addressed to children reminded them that 'If a peece of pie or of tart, be offered thee, receive that on thy plate or trencher, and not with thy fingers.' In 1853 ladies were advised:

> It is an affectation of ultra-fashion to eat pie with a fork, and has a very awkward and inconvenient look. Cut it up first with your knife and fork both; then proceed to eat it with the fork in your right hand . . . At a public table, a lady should never volunteer to dress salad for others of the company. Neither should she cut up a pie, and help it round. These things ought only to be done by a gentleman, or a servant.

The Social Life of Pies

In modern society, where anyone in theory can make money, it is difficult to appreciate that once upon a time wealth was tied absolutely to social class, and therefore social class

Victorian illustration of a pigeon pie. Note the pigeons' feet.

determined what you ate, even to the extent of determining the type of pastry making up your pie. Farming and household manuals of the seventeenth and eighteenth centuries clearly instructed that the piecrust for the master's family be made from the finest wheat flour, whereas for the servants' piecrust the second milling of wheat or barley was to be used, or maslin (a mix of wheat and rye) or rye.

Game pies and many fish pies by definition could only be enjoyed by those who had the land and the hunting rights. The poor and the working class of Victorian England got mutton pies (if they were lucky), with meat from sheep past their prime, or beef pies from old dairy or draft animals. An English newspaper article of 1857 about the famous Derby horse race meeting summed up the class-food divide nicely:

> The Derby is worth seeing. I do not know where England altogether, is so well represented. It is there in samples – the highest aristocracy and the lowest democracy . . . The

Supper Dishes.

Mayonnaise of Salmon

Raised Pie.

Lobster Salad.

Cherry Tartlets.

Game Pie.

Fancy Pastry.

Open Tart.

Tomato and Cucumber Salad.

Ratafia Pudding.

Pigeon Pie.

Meat Pie.

'Supper Dishes', from *Mrs Beeton's Everyday Cookery*.

Bishops drive out in their coaches with hampers of game pies and champagne; and the costermonger, loaded with bread, cheese and beer, drives out with his barrow and donkey.

In England, pigeon pies were high-status pies for high-status people because only wealthy landowners could maintain pigeon cotes to supply fresh meat over winter. In America the situation was initially the reverse. Early in the nineteenth century vast flocks of passenger pigeons, several miles across, would literally darken the sky. The birds were freely and extraordinarily easily available for anyone with a gun and a craving for pigeon pie dinner. So successful were the hunters that the passenger pigeon became extinct by 1914, but in the small hiatus before their end, when they were a rarity, they briefly became expensive restaurant food for the wealthy.

The dynasty of pies had its own hierarchical order on the eighteenth-century dining table. At that time meals were served in the style that came to be called *à la française* (as distinct from the style we use today, service *à la russe*, in which individual dishes are served sequentially to guests). Two or more courses would each consist of a variety of dishes set out simultaneously on the table with geometric precision and an eye for symmetry. Pies were very important in this style of service, as they had impressive visual 'presence' on the table. Grand pies often formed the centrepiece, with smaller pies at the sides and corners (some were actually called 'corner pies'). The range of possible pie fillings at this time in history was truly amazing.

4
Filling Stuff

Good apple pies are a considerable part of our
domestic happiness.

Jane Austen

The *Oxford English Dictionary* gives one definition of 'stuff'
as 'materials for filling a pie'. It does not attempt to list the
various materials – nor could it, as almost everything imaginable from the sublime to the sinister has at some time or
other found its way into a pie.

The original pie, as we have seen, contained single large
pieces of meat. By the fourteenth century the range of
fillings had broadened to include fruit, delicate custards and
finely minced and spiced meats. One thing that strikes us
today when we look at recipes of this era is that many of the
'savoury' dishes contain sugar. The distinction between
sweet and savoury food is a relatively modern one; medieval
cooks knew no such distinction. Sugar was an expensive
imported ingredient and was used in the same way as a spice.
It became cheaper with the opening up of sugar refineries in
Britain in the mid-sixteenth century, and cheaper still with
the development of the East India trade in the seventeenth
century.

Detail from *A Table of Desserts* (1640) by Jan Davidsz. De Heem.

By the mid-seventeenth century, sugar was not used sparingly as a spice, but in quantities that clearly imply a taste for sweetness. The famous bestselling seventeenth-century cookbook *The Accomplish't Cook* by Robert May included this fascinating recipe for herring pie:

To make minced Herring Pies

Take salt herrings being watered, crush them between your hands, and you shall loose the fish from the skin, take off the skin whole, and lay them in a dish; then have a pound of almond paste ready, mince the herrings, and stamp them with the almond paste, two of the milts or rows, five or six dates, some grated manchet, sugar, sack, rose-water and saffron, make the composition somewhat stiff, and fill the skins, put butter in the bottom of your pie, lay on the herring, and on them dates and gooseberries, currants, barberries, and butter, close it up and bake it, being baked with butter, verjuyce, and sugar.

By the eighteenth century the distinction between savoury and sweet dishes was becoming clearer, and many cookbooks of the time gave two versions of meat pies to cater for alternative taste preferences. This recipe from Hannah Glasse's *The Art of Cookery, Made Plain and Easy* (1747) was followed by the savoury alternative.

To make a very fine Sweet Lamb or Veal Pye

Season your Lamb with Salt, Pepper, Cloves, Mace and Nutmeg, all beat fine, to your Palate. Cut your Lamb, or Veal, into little Pieces, make a good Puff-paste Crust, lay it into your Dish, then lay in your Meat, strew on it some stoned Raisins and Currants clean washed, and some Sugar; then lay on it some Forced meat Balls made sweet, and in the Summer some Artichoke Bottoms boiled, and scalded Grapes in the Winter. Boil Spanish Potatoes cut in Pieces, candied Citron, candied Orange and Lemon-peel, and three or four large Blades of Mace; put Butter on the Top, close up your Pye, and bake it. Have ready against it comes out of the Oven a Caudle made thus: Take a Pint of White Wine, and mix in the Yolks of three Eggs, stir it well together over the Fire, one Way, all the Time till it is thick; then take it off, stir in Sugar enough to sweeten it, and squeeze in the Juice of a Lemon; pour it hot into your Pye, and close it up again. Send it hot to Table.

Tiny pies from Pézenas in the south of France, showing their typical shape.

Minced meat, spices, sugar, dried fruit — there are medieval echoes to be heard in this recipe, and they can still be heard in our Christmas mince pies. The echo persists more strongly in, of all places, a little town called Pézenas in the Languedoc region of France. A local speciality is its *petits pâtés de Pézenas* — tiny, bite-sized plant-pot-shaped pies with a sweet lamb filling. The legendary Lord Clive of India stayed in Pézenas for several months in 1786 and, in spite of poor health, led a busy social life. Locals were intrigued by the pies served at his home, and prevailed upon his cooks for the recipe. Once they became a local speciality, the pies became immutable to change and endured like culinary time-capsules, giving us a glimpse into a previous era. A similar thing happened in Nova Scotia to the Cape Breton pork pie, which contains no pork — but has dates where pork presumably used to be.

Fish Pies

Fish is a perfectly good alternative to meat as a pie filling – if you have a choice, that is. For many periods in history, meat-less days were mandated by the Church (and often backed by statute law) and at some periods these added up to almost half the days on the calendar. Fish pies took on a great significance on these days, particularly for grand occasions.

There were a number of reasons for decreeing abstention from meat. In ancient times meat was thought to inflame the passions (thereby distracting the mind from higher thoughts) whereas fish (or rather, creatures that lived in the water, which included whales and 'porpuses') were seen as cooling. It was also believed that the characteristics or habits of everything in the natural world would be transmitted to the eater, so the fact that fish did not have an obvious sex life added to its suitability for days of religious observance. In later periods the rules were reinforced for non-religious reasons: agricultural ('by the eating of fish, much flesh is saved to the country'), economic (the fishing industry was encouraged) and political (a good fishing industry provided expertise and manpower for the navy and for voyages of exploration).

It was perfectly possible, of course, to obey the letter of the meatless law without actually being abstemious if one was so inclined. There was nothing *maigre* about some of the grand fish dishes produced for fast days. The author of *The Compleat Cook* (1658) gave a recipe for carp pie enriched with the blood of the carp and the flesh of a fat eel, and ended with the comment that 'this is meat for a Pope'. A French cookbook of 1702 provided the following recipe – surely the ultimate in fish pie exotica – but nevertheless quite correct for a day of abstinence:

Medieval kitchen with a large rabble of people and several examples of pies and pasties.

A Pan-pie made of Carps-roes and Tongues

The Tongues and Roes of the Carps must be laid in order upon a piece of fine Paste, in the bottom of the Pan; season'd with Pepper, Salt, Nutmeg, fine Herbs, Chibbols, Morilles, common Mushrooms, Truffles and sweet Butter. Then, all being cover'd with a Lid of the same Paste, let the Pie be bak'd with a gently Fire, and serv'd up with Lemmon-juice.

During the 40 days of Lent in the Christian calendar, fish was also forbidden, and at certain periods of history, so were dairy products and eggs. Pie-cooks of the time became very creative with substitutions such as almond milk and rice, nuts and fruits – and the corpus of pie recipes is the greater for their efforts.

Sweet Pies

If you are one of those sweet-toothed souls to whom 'pie' means a dessert, you have probably been frustrated up to now as meat pies have dominated our story. Your time is now come.

Fruit pies started to come into their own during the sixteenth century as sugar became cheaper and more delicate forms of pastry were available. It is not that fruit was absent from pies before this time – far from it – but it was rarely a primary ingredient. The first predominantly fruit pies were still called 'bake-metes' ('meat' in its old sense of any solid food), but these were not fruit pies as we now know them, and not just because of the thick coffin-crust. One medieval recipe for a 'bake-mete' of pears instructs that 'gobbets of marrow' (bone marrow, not vegetable) be placed between the pieces of fruit and in another the apple is flavoured with saffron:

For To Make Tartys In Applis

Tak gode Applys and gode Spycis and Figys and reysons and Perys and wan they are wel ybrayed colourd wyth Safroun wel and do yt in a cofyn and do yt forth to bake wel.

There is one other historic fruit pie that deserves special mention: a pie made from an exotic, imported and therefore expensive fruit candied with expensive sugar. Orengeado is candied orange peel, and it was enormously popular from Elizabethan times until well into the eighteenth century. A pie made from orengeado, perhaps layered with apples, was a very expensive delicacy. A pie fit for a queen, it seems, as two of the master pastry-cooks of

Apple pies and strudel.

Elizabeth I were proud to make New Year gifts of an orengeado pie to her in 1600.

We have been careless with our pie repertoire. The demise of apple-pear pie with figs and saffron and orengeado pies are tragic losses. What did we replace them with? Dessert pies have moved well beyond fruit and custard, and the line is blurred between pies and cakes with some pies resembling cakes with a crust (pecan pie springs to mind). Some sweet pies are even made with vegetables.

Vegetable Pies

Vegetable pies are not absent from historic cookbooks, but the importance and role of vegetables in the diet has changed significantly over the centuries. Aside from the members of some religious orders who abstained from it, our medieval ancestors would have found it incomprehensible that an individual would freely choose not to eat meat. High-protein food was too hard to come by, especially in the European winter, and there was never too much.

There are some fine vegetable pies in old cookbooks, although as with fruit pies they are not necessarily strictly 'vegetarian' (a relatively modern word), often containing marrow from bones where we might use butter, such as in this recipe from about 1720.

An Artichoke Pye

Take ye bottomes of 6 or 8 artichokes being boyld & sliced season ym wth sweet spice mix ym wth ye marrow of 3 bones wth citron & lemon piele oringoe roots damsons gooseberries & grap[e]s citron lemon butter & close ye pye: A Skarrot or a Potatoe pye is made ye same way.

Vegetable pies were not always 'savoury' dishes. The traditional Thanksgiving pumpkin pie has an old lineage. There are seventeenth-century recipes for 'pompion pie' (pompion is an old name for pumpkin) and other intrinsically sweet vegetables such as sweet potato and skirret (a member of the carrot family) have long been used as pie fillings. The sweet–savoury combination applied to 'vegetable' pies too. William Ellis's farming and household manual from 1750 has a recipe for an 'onion pie' that is half onion and half apple, with no indication as to which ingredient was the substitute for a dearth in the other, and no clue as to when it was eaten.

Those who do not choose vegetarianism (or veganism, an even newer word) may have it thrust upon them. Peasants in most societies, the faithful during Lent and the general population during wartime do not choose. Cooks have two

Pumpkin pie.

basic options when faced with absent or forbidden ingredients: embrace the alternative wholeheartedly and with creativity, or aim to make the substitute look and taste as close to the real thing as possible (and tell, or not.) During the Second World War in Britain, economies had to be made with wheat, and meat was rationed, so whither that staple of the working man's dinner, pie? Frederick Marquis, first Earl of Woolton, was appointed Minister of Food in Britain in 1940, and charged with the job of organizing the rationing programme. He managed a seemingly impossible feat by doing the job brilliantly and at the same time becoming enormously popular with the British public. A recipe for a vegetable pie to serve on meatless days was named after him, and described as being 'on the outside exactly like a steak and kidney pie, and on the inside just like a steak and kidney pie – without the steak and kidney'. The celebrity testimonial was a propaganda triumph rather than a culinary one, but do judge for yourself.

Woolton Pie

Take 1lb each diced of potatoes, cauliflower, swedes, and carrots, three or four spring onions – if possible, one teaspoonful of vegetable extract, and one tablespoonful of oatmeal. Cook all together for 10 minutes with just enough water to cover. Stir occasionally to prevent the mixture from sticking. Allow to cool; put into a piedish, sprinkle with chopped parsley, and cover with a crust of potato or wheatmeal pastry. Bake in a moderate oven until the pastry is nicely browned and serve hot with a brown gravy.

Vegetable pies do not need to be apologetic alternatives to meat, however, as the slightly mysterious Frenchman Baron Brisse in his cookbook of 1868 showed with a recipe for a vegetable pie in the form of an open tart divided into sections by strips of paste, each section filled with a different-coloured vegetable. As he pointed out, this 'not only pleases the palate, but the eye, and is a great addition to our fast day dinners'.

Frugal Pies

The domestic art of economy has been prized by cookbook writers for centuries. It was summed up nicely by the American author Lydia Maria Child in her book *The Frugal Housewife: Dedicated to Those Who Are Not Ashamed of Economy* (1830):

The true economy of housekeeping is simply the art of gathering up all the fragments, so that nothing be lost

. . . Nothing should be thrown away so long as it is possible to make any use of it, however trifling that use may be.

By their very nature pies are an eminently suitable device for practising this art, but it can perhaps be taken too far, as Charles Dickens graphically described in *Our Mutual Friend*:

When dinner was done, and when what remained of the platters and what remained of the congealed gravy had been put back into what remained of the pie, which served as an economical investment for all miscellaneous savings, Riderhood filled the mug with beer and took a long drink.

Dickens's American contemporary, Nathaniel Hawthorne was not too sure about pies either, at least the English hotel version, where 'sometimes, perhaps, a meat-pie, which, if you eat it, weighs upon your conscience, with the idea that you have eaten the scraps of other people's dinners'.

Pies such as these – repositories of a week's leftovers – were once so commonplace as to earn their own names. I advise you to have no illusions as to the content of Scrap pies, Saturday pies or Old Maid pies.

Frugality (short of parsimony, that is) may well be a domestic virtue, but there have always been many for whom it is a necessity. Surely the most frugal pie of all, for the poorest folk of all, was the Burr Pye. An early eighteenth-century manual 'for the improvement of husbandry and trade' described the butchering of an animal and the sending of the hides to market 'where poor women . . . also cut off some bits of flesh that lie by the horns, called *burrs*, with these are made pyes.'

Sometimes frugality must be practised on a national scale. During the Second World War there was a drive in the

Carrying a
Christmas pie.

United States to cut wheat consumption by 40 per cent
and fat by 20 per cent, and one of the requests made of
American housewives was that they made 'coverless' pies.
The severe wheat shortages that occurred in England in the
eighteenth century had a couple of interesting long-term
results. The pie, as we have seen, was important for its
'presence' on the dining table. To compensate for their lack
when wheat was scarce the great pottery manufacturers

A Second World
War advertise-
ment for
Marmite.

designed dishes with a golden glaze and scalloped edges to
mimic the structure of a pie – so-called piecrust ware.
These 'crock pies' were early versions of pot pies. Another
positive outcome was that the crustless fillings developed
independent lives and went on to be served as terrines, pup-
tons and pâté.

Cheating Pies and Sinister Pies

There is a mystery inherent in a pie by virtue of its contents
being hidden beneath its crust. The mystery is both its promise and its curse. We want a pleasant surprise, not a nasty

shock. The big question, when the pie is broached, is whether we are opening Pandora's box or a treasure chest. Meat pies are the real worry here. The meat pie is the point at which many of the fine lines between frugality, harmless deception and sinister intent can meet. Happily, the law is there to protect us.

Australian law says that a meat pie must contain a minimum of 25 per cent meat, which hardly sounds sufficient. The real anxiety starts when you know that this can include snouts, ears, tendons, blood and blood vessels and a whole lot of other animal parts (but not foetuses or offal, which is possibly reassuring). In fact, as the method of testing for meat actually tests for protein, it would be perfectly possible for a pie made of congealed thickened blood to pass the meat test.

BOW[wow]ERY PIES.

CHINAMAN.—"Oh, gr'at Countree this. Good Man you—Good Pie you give me—Mut-ton you only call him, but he real bow-wow, what you call Dog."

Bow[wow]ery pies: a cartoon which plays on the common fear that the contents of a pie may not be what is advertised, and which is also a racial slur.

The Accident in Lombard St, 1787, by Charles Willson Peale.

There is a different set of motives at work at the domestic level when a host serves up one food as another, perhaps with the intent to deceive. Presumably this is intended to impress the guest, in which case the deception had better be good and remain undiscovered. Samuel Pepys dined at the home of his cousin on 6 January 1660 and was clearly unimpressed as 'the venison pasty was palpable beef, which was not handsome'. On another occasion he ate a venison pasty 'which proved a pasty of salted pork'. Cookbooks of the seventeenth and eighteenth centuries frequently contained recipes for cooking beef to mimic venison, so one has to assume that this was common practice at the time.

Fruit pies can deceive too. One does hear occasional rumours in Australia of 'apple' pies being made entirely from choko (chayote), for example, but at least the substitute is also from the plant kingdom. For sheer marketing nerve it is hard to beat the Ritz cracker manufacturers in the 1930s, who for many years proudly displayed a recipe for

Mock Apple Pie on the package. The pie filling was made entirely from crackers, and difficult though it may be to believe, it was popular to the extent of becoming almost a cult item. It is even more difficult to believe the many fans who swore it was indistinguishable from the real thing.

The idea of fake fruit pies pale into insignificance in comparison to that of meat pies made from diseased or fake meat, and there is worse in the world than 'meat' pies filled with snouts and tails. And I don't mean the 'covered uncertainties' with the 'feline character' sold by street vendors in Victorian England and described by Albert Smith in *Sketches of London Life and Character* (1849). There is something much worse called called 'mechanically retrieved meat' – that is, 'meat' scraped off carcasses and used in burgers and pies. A sort of reddish paste suspected of spreading Mad Cow Disease – and you don't get much more sinister than that. Or do you?

A primal fear – one which has fed many a literary tale and many an urban myth – is that of being fed human flesh in a pie. Shakespeare used this gruesome idea as the ultimate weapon of revenge in his extraordinarily bloodthirsty play, *Titus Andronicus*. Titus is a Roman general who kills the remaining two sons of his enemy Tamora, Queen of the Goths, and has their flesh made into 'two mighty pies' which unknowingly, she eats. The tale of Sweeney Todd, the London barber who slits the throats of his customers and has them made into pies by his paramour to be sold to her own customers, has horrified and thrilled readers and audiences for a century or so, and may be loosely based on a factual murder that took place in 1785 in the same city.

History is littered with stories of cannibalism during times of great hardship and famine, and as much as we are revolted by the idea, we are also fascinated. What does

A baker with a tray of pies, engraved from William Hogarth's *March to Finchley* (1750).

human flesh taste like? Pork, the myths say. Perhaps this is why pork was used in the 'mermaid pie' that was so popular in the seventeenth and early eighteenth centuries. Mermaids were a source of great fascination at that time, with great scientific interest in supposed sightings. There was a vigorous debate among some clergy as to whether or not eating mermaids (who were half human after all) amounted to

Sinister pies, the meat provided by the Demon Barber of Fleet Street, from the film *Sweeney Todd* (2007).

cannibalism. A recipe for mermaid pie appears, essentially unchanged, in cookbooks for over a century. Here is one version, from William Salmon's *The Family-Dictionary, or, Houshold Companion* (1695):

Mermaid-Pye

Take a Pig, scald it, and bone it; and having dried it well with a Cloath, season it with beaten Nutmeg, Pepper, and chop'd Sage; then take two Neats-Tongues; when dried and cold after boiling, and slice them in lengths, and as thick as a Half-Crown, and lay a quarter of your Pig in a square or round Pye, and the slices of the Tongue on it; then another quarter, and more Tongue: and thus do four times double, and lay over all these some slices of Bacon, scatter a few Cloves, put in some pieces of Butter and Bay-leaves, then bake it; and when it is so, fill it up with pieces of sweet Butter, and make your Past white of the Butter and Flower. This Pig, or Mermaid-Pye, so called, is to be eaten cold.

On an entirely different note, there is a type of pie strongly associated with Scotland which has aesthetic and health dangers that justify its inclusion here amongst the sinister pies. It is the Fried Pie – which is just what it says, a baked pie cooked a second time by frying. Scotland is not called the Land of the Brave for nothing.

5
Special Occasion Pies

Methinks a Feast is not well set forth if there bee
no Pies or bak'd meates.
John Taylor (1578–1653)

Practical, versatile, universally esteemed and provided with its own edible, easily decorated gift box of pastry – small wonder that the pie still plays a feature role at many of our favourite celebrations, so much so that it is often symbolic of the very event itself.

Christmas Pie

In the beginning, there was frumenty – a plain wheat porridge that was the staple food of peasants and a side dish to venison for the rich. It was enriched for special occasions (such as Christmas) with sugar and spice and all other things nice, such as eggs, dried fruit ('plums'), wine and finely chopped meat. This Christmas porridge (or pottage) eventually evolved into Christmas (mincemeat) pie when it was cooked in a coffin, Christmas pudding when it was cooked in a cloth and Christmas cake when it was cooked in a shaped metal tin.

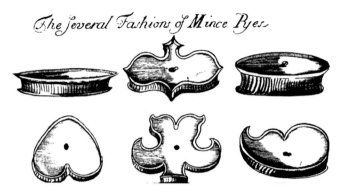

The several Fashions of Mince Pyes

From Henry Howard, *England's Newest Way in All Sorts of Cookery, Pastry . . .* (1708).

The mince(meat) pie may have lost its meat, and its other ingredients may now be freely available all year round, but it has not lost its association with Christmas. Seventeenth-century Puritans tried hard to ban it (calling it 'idolatrie in crust') but they did not succeed: the Christmas mince pie lives. Not so another famous Christmas pie – a grand pie, a pie in the coffin style, a pie solid with the finest meat. The most famous of all came from Yorkshire, and the earliest recipe is from Hannah Glasse's *Art of Cookery*:

To make a Yorkshire Christmas Pye

First make a good Standing Crust, let the Wall and Bottom be very thick; bone a Turky, a Goose, a Fowl, a Partridge, and a Pigeon, season them all very well, take Half an Ounce of Mace, and Half and Ounce of Nutmegs, a Quarter of an Ounce of Cloves, and Half an Ounce of Black Pepper, all beat fine together, two large Spoonfuls of Salt, and then mix them together. Open the Fowls all down the Back, and bone them, first the Pigeon, then the Partridge, cover them; then the Fowl, then the

Goose, and then the Turky, which must be large: season them all well first, and lay them in the Crust so as it will look only like a whole Turky; then have a Hare ready cased, and wiped with a clean Cloth. Cut it to Pieces, that is, joint, season it, and lay it as close as you can on one side, and on the other Side, Woodcock, more Game, and what Sort of wild Fowl you can get. Season them well, and lay them close; put at least four Pounds of Butter in the Pye, then lay on your Lid, which must be a very thick one, and let it be well baked. It must have a very hot Oven, and will take at least four Hours.

This Crust will take a Bushel of Flour; in this Chapter, you will see how to make it. These Pies are often sent to London in a Box as Presents; therefore the Walls must be well built.

Thanksgiving

America has developed a pie tradition unequivocally and unapologetically at the sweet end of the scale, and at no time is this better demonstrated than at Thanksgiving in November. It seems that the country goes pie-mad at this time, and the traditional pies reflect that this is harvest season. Regional differences are inevitable of course, and the food writer Clementine Paddleford claimed to have summarized them in the 1950s when she said, 'Tell me where your grandmother came from and I can tell you how many kinds of pie you serve for Thanksgiving.' If she was from the Midwest, Ms Paddleford said, there would be two types (mince and pumpkin), if from New England, three (mince, pumpkin, cranberry), Boston, four (mince, pumpkin, cranberry and apple). Ms Paddleford excluded the West for reasons

Thanksgiving pies.

she did not explain, and the South on the rather controversial basis that pie was not favoured there.

There is no mention of savoury pies anywhere in any discussion of Thanksgiving. The American preoccupation with sweet dessert pies is absolute – an interesting point which we will explore further in chapter Six.

Village Pies

Every English village seems to have a particular day when some local tradition is celebrated – and the celebratory food is often pie. A few stellar examples must suffice. On Easter

Monday in the village of Hallaton in Leicestershire, for ancient and forgotten reasons, the local parson is obliged to provide his congregation with a hare pie after the morning service. The remains of the pie are then taken to a field called Hare Pie Bank on the outskirts of the village, to be tossed to the crowd before the unruly traditional game of bottle-kicking begins.

In the fishing village of Mousehole in Cornwall it is traditional to eat 'stargazy pie' on the evening of 23 December. It is an intriguing pie, made with pilchards placed so that their heads poke through the crust at the centre of the pie, gazing at the stars, as it were. It is made in honour of a local mythical hero, Tom Bawcock ('bawcock' is an old word meaning 'a fine fellow'), whom legend says set out on a bad night during a bad season, returning with sufficient fish to save the locals from starvation.

A traditional Stargazy Pie from Cornwall, with the heads of the fish poking out through the crust.

The folk of Lapford in Devon used to tuck into 'pestle pies' on the feast day of the Translation of St Thomas Becket (7 July). A 'pestle' is the leg (thigh) of an animal, and a pestle pie is a large 'standing' pie which 'contains a whole gammon, and sometimes a neat's tongue also, together with a couple of fowls, and if a turkey not the worse'. The local church dedicated to the saint was built in the twelfth century by a local nobleman as penance for his part in the Archbishop's murder in 1170, but how this is connected to gammon pies is, to say the least, obscure.

Obligatory Pies

It was not uncommon in times gone by for items of food to be given as symbolic gifts or token payments, and pies were ideal as they could be impressive, extravagant and would keep and transport well.

The city of Gloucester, by ancient custom, presented a lamprey pie to the sovereign at Christmas time, as a token of loyalty. Lampreys are scaleless freshwater sucker-fish resembling eels, desirable in the past for their oily, gamey flesh. The tradition of gifting lamprey pies to the royal family continued until the end of Queen Victoria's reign, but was revived for the coronation of Queen Elizabeth II in 1953 when a 42-pound pie was cooked by the RAF catering corps.

The number 24 pops up regularly in pie history, and folklorists continue to debate the meaning of the nursery rhyme 'four-and-twenty blackbirds baked in a pie'. A 'double dozen' is a significant number in many cultures, not least as the number of herring pies present on symbolic gifting occasions. The reasons behind this are difficult to explain.

'Sing a song of sixpence, a pocketful of rye
Four-and-twenty blackbirds baked in a pie
When the pie was opened the birds began to sing
Wasn't that a dainty dish to set before the king?'

The choice of herring pies themselves is more obvious: they were desirable because they kept well, were rich (oily) and were suitable for fast days. The town of Yarmouth, famous for its herrings, was required by ancient charter to send 24 herring pies to the king each year, and the Sheriffs of Norwich had the same obligation at Lent to their local Lord of Caister.

A final example is of an individual obligation. A shepherd family called Edwards lived for centuries in a small cottage in the parish of the church of St Constantine in Harlyn, Cornwall. The annual rent was a single limpet pie (with raisins and herbs), due on 9 March, the feast day of the saint. It was a cheap rent indeed as limpets were food for the poor – freely available from the tide-line.

Bride Pie

Before there was wedding cake, there was bride pie. Bride pie did not give rise to the modern wedding cake, which materialized from the same path that led to Christmas cake. Bride pie was an entirely different entity. Initially there was no specific recipe and there were no mandatory ingredients; it was simply a pie containing the best delicacies that could be procured at the time. Such a pie was often called a 'batalia pie', the name coming from *beatilles*, meaning beautiful little things – things such as cocks' combs, lambs' stones (testicles) and goose giblets. The origin of the name was clearly lost upon cooks, who thought that it referred to battlements, and consequently often constructed batalia pies in the form of castles, complete with turrets. With or without turrets, it was a pie entirely suitable for a celebration, and some early recipes for batalia pie specified that it was suitable for a bride's pie.

The most amazing bride's pie recipe comes from the cookbook of Robert May, *The Accomplish't Cook*. The seventeenth century was the pinnacle of English pie-making, and this pie was the absolute zenith:

To make an extraordinary Pie, or a Bride Pie, of severall Compounds, being several distinct Pies on one bottom.

Provide cock-stones and combs, or lamb-stones and sweet-breads of veal, a little set in hot water and cut to pieces; also two or three oxe pallets blanched and slic't, a pint of oysters, sliced dates, a handful of pine kernels, a little quantity of broom-buds pickled, some fine inter-larded bacon sliced, nine or ten chestnuts roasted and blanched, season them with the salt, nutmeg, and some large mace, and close it up with some butter. For the cau-dle, beat up some butter, with three yolks of eggs, some white wine or claret wine, the juyce of a lemon or two, cut up the lid, and pour on the lear, shaking it well together, then lay on the meat, slic't lemon, and pickled barberries, and cover it again, let these Ingredients be put into the middle or scollops of the Pie.

Several other Pies belong to the first form, but you must be sure to make the three fashions proportionably answering one the other; you may set them on one bot-tom of paste, which will be more convenient; or if you set them several you may bake the middle one of flour, it being baked and cold, take out the flour in the bottom, and put in live birds, or a snake, which will seem strange to the beholders, which cut up the Pie at the table. This is onely for a Wedding to pass away time.

Now for the other Pies you may fill them with sev-eral Ingredients, as in one you may put oysters, being parboild and bearded, season them with large mace, pepper, some beaten ginger, and salt, season them light-ly, and fill the Pie, then lay on marrow and some good butter, close it up and bake it. Then make a lear for it with white wine, the oyster liquor, three or four oysters bruised in pieces to make it stronger, but take out the pieces, and an onion, or rub the bottom of the dish with a clove of garlick; it being boild, put in a piece of butter, with a lemon, sweet hearbs will be good boild in it, bound up fast together; cut up the lid, or make a hole to let the lear in, &c.

Another you may make of Prawns and Cockles, being seasoned as the first, but no marrow: a few pickled mushrooms (if you have them) it being baked, beat up a piece of butter, a little vinegar, a slic'd nutmeg, and the juyce of two or three oranges thick, and pour it into the Pie.

A third you may make a Bird Pie; take young Birds, as larks, pulled and drawn, and a force meat to put in the bellies made of grated bread, sweet herbs minced very small, beef suet, or marrow minced, almonds beat with a little cream to keep them from oyling, a little parmisan (or none) or old cheese; season this meat with nutmeg, ginger, and salt; then mix them together with cream and eggs like a pudding, stuff the larks with it, then season the larks with nutmeg, pepper, and salt, and lay them in the Pie, put in some butter, and scatter between them pine-kernels, yolks of eggs, and sweet herbs, the eggs and herbs being minced very small; being baked make a lear with the juice of oranges and butter beat up thick, and shaken well together.

For another of the Pies, you may boil artichocks, and take onely the bottoms for the Pie, cut them into quarters or less, and season them with nutmeg. Thus with several Ingredients you may fill up the other Pies.

Weddings inevitably lead to families, and many family events in the past were deemed worthy of a special pie (or cake). We no longer make 'groaning pies' – the pies to feed attendants and visitors at 'groaning time' (an old but apt name for childbirth) or christening pies, but 'funeral pies' are still known amongst the Pennsylvania Dutch. They are otherwise known as raisin (or rosina) pies, on account of their main ingredient, chosen perhaps because they are always available, and the pies travel well.

Giant Pies

Culinary history is littered with stories of supersize pies, and many of these have been Christmas pies. If you thought Mrs Glasse's pie was big, how about the one prepared in 1826 by Mr Roberts, victualler in Sheffield? It was 'composed of rabbits, veal, and pork, in such quantities, as to weigh, before being carried to the oven, 15 stones 10 pounds'. An even bigger one was made in 1835 by Mrs Kirk, of the Old Ship Inn, Rotherham, 'which when taken to the oven, weighed upwards of seventeen stone; it consists of one rump of beef, two legs of veal, two legs of pork, three hares, three couple of rabbits, three geese, two brace of pheasants, four brace of partridges, two turkeys, two couple of fowls, with 7½ stone of best flour.'

The citizens of the tiny Yorkshire village of Denby Dale know a thing or two about giant pies: they have been making them for over 200 years. The first was made in 1788 to celebrate the recovery of King George III from one of his bouts of madness. The second was made in 1815 to celebrate the victory at Waterloo in 1815 and the third in 1846 to celebrate the repeal of the Corn Laws. Two pies were made in 1877 for Queen Victoria's jubilee. The first (made by professional bakers), which weighed one and a half tons, was embarrassingly unfit for consumption due to the meat being 'off', and was quickly buried; the 'Resurrection Pie' was made (by local housewives) a month later. In 1928 a pie was made to raise hospital funds; this one was 16 feet long by 5 feet wide by 15 inches deep; the pastry required 1,120 pounds of flour and 200 pounds of lard, and there were 1,500 pounds of potatoes and the meat of six bullocks in the filling. The 1964 pie was also a fundraiser, to build a village hall. The Denby Dale Bicentenary Pie, made in 1988, measured 20 feet long, 7 feet wide and 18 inches deep. The most recent pie in 2000 was a triple celebration: the 12-tonne Millennium Pie also acknowledged the Queen Mother's 100th birthday and the 150th anniversary of the local railway line.

Entertainment Pies

It could be argued that there is an element of entertainment in every pie, as every pie is inherently a surprise by virtue of its crust. The medieval 'chastlete' – the pie in the style of a castle (page 48) would have been great fun – and great eating – but there are some pies in an entirely different league that are clearly meant to entertain, and just as clearly *not meant to be eaten*. These pies depend for their success on the anticipatory delight that is the right of every pie-eater. A sixteenth-century Italian recipe will serve to illustrate:

> ### To make Pies that the Birds may be alive in them, and flie out when it is cut up
>
> Make the coffin of a great pie or pastry, in the bottome thereof make a hole as big as your fist, or bigger if you will, let the sides of the coffin bee somewhat higher then

Ordinary pies, which done put it full of flower [flour] and bake it, and being baked, open the hole in the bottome, and take out the flower. Then having a Pie of the bigness of the hole in the bottome of the coffin aforesaid, you shal put it into the coffin, withall put into the said coffin round about the aforesaid pie as many small live birds as the empty coffin will hold, besides the pie aforesaid. And this is to be done at such time as you send the Pie to the table, and set before the guests: where uncovering or cutting up the lid of the great Pie, all the birds will flie out, which is to delight and pleasure shew to the company. And because they shall not bee altogether mocked, you shall cut open the small Pie, and in this sort you may make many others, the like you may do with a tart.

This idea of live birds flying out of a pie to give delight and pleasure to the guests was popular for centuries. Robert May (the author of *The Accomplish't Cook*) went one better with instructions for an incredibly complex pie/pastry construction that also contained frogs which, when released, would 'make the ladies to skip and shreek'.

The concept was taken several leaps further at a time not at all concerned with political correctness. Jeffrey Hudson was born in 1619, and at the age of nine years he stood only 18 inches tall (although 'gracefully proportioned'.) He went on to live an incredibly exciting life, fighting duels, being captured by pirates and spending time as a political prisoner, but he first came to fame as the surprise ingredient in a pie in 1626. The lucky and very amused recipients were Charles I and his wife Henrietta Maria, who immediately 'adopted' (i.e., made a pet of) him.

Another interpretation of the same theme occurred in New York in 1895. A select group of gentlemen in that city were invited to a secret dinner and a mysterious treat was suggested. The treat turned out to be a pie containing a cloud of canaries – quickly followed by sixteen-year-old Susie Johnson, wearing nothing very substantial. What happened next has never been authenticated but, needless to say, the general public (who were not invited) were outraged at the whole concept of a 'Pie Girl Dinner'.

6
Around the World with Pie

Do not dismiss the dish saying that it is just, simply food.
The blessed thing is an entire civilization in itself.
Abdulhak Sinasi

We humans are constantly on the move around the world
and when we migrate we take our eating habits with us. We
do so to use our agricultural and culinary knowledge, and
because eating familiar food maintains our link with home
and eases our homesickness. We may have to substitute
ingredients and adapt our cooking methods, but even after
several generations, our heritage is still evident in the food
we serve at home.

When Europeans started to spread beyond their traditional homelands, they took their grain-based cuisine with
them, and attempted to make familiar types of bread and
pastry. By the seventeenth century, England was at its peak
in both its maritime powers and its culinary skill, and as
England's empire developed, its pies went with it, to be
adapted according to local ingredients and conditions.

The two great waves of migration from pie-loving Britain
– to the Americas starting in the early seventeenth century,
and to Australia in the late eighteenth century – produced

Pie-eating contest, USA, 4 July 1945.

two great pie-loving nations. What is interesting is that, in spite of this common origin, the pie portfolios of these two ex-colonies are very different. In America, the unqualified word 'pie' unequivocally means a sweet dessert item, whereas in Australia it just as certainly means a *meat* pie.

Nowhere is this divide better demonstrated than in the pie competitions in both countries. The American Pie Council's Annual National Pie Championship has twelve to fourteen categories, all sweet (always apple, fruit/berry, cream, citrus, custard, pumpkin, sweet potato, nut, chocolate cream and peanut butter, plus a variable few others.) By way of contrast, the Great Aussie Pie Competition (for commercial bakers) in 2006 had five categories only: red meat, poultry, game, fish, vegetarian – not a spoonful of sugar anywhere.

So, we have two countries divided by a common culinary heritage. How might this have come about?

America

The first mass migrants to North America – the Puritans and Pilgrims – arrived with the intention and equipment to be small farmers, and the area they chose to settle proved to be excellent for their purpose. In particular the apple so beloved in old England grew wonderfully well in New England, and within a few decades it was a staple. Dried apples became a standard provision for the long overland journeys to the West, and were used for one major purpose – apple pies.

It was a different story with the wheat crops in those early years. As the early settlers finally learned from the Native Americans, this was corn (maize) country, and not suitable for wheat. Wheat was not grown on a massive scale until the West was well and truly won, by which time Americans had learned to be sparing with it – and a small amount of wheat goes further if it is used to make pies rather than bread.

William Henry Shelton's painting of foraging Confederate soldiers taking homemade pies from an enemy farmhouse during a raid, c. 1863.

The pie as national metaphor: a cartoon showing an Englishman (probably the gluttonous George III) gobbling up a pie representing France. He is about to eat up Napoleon Bonaparte. From an etching by George M. Woodward, 1803.

BUONAPARTÉ PIE.

It is hardly surprising that to this day New England is considered to be the pie capital of America, whose inhabitants traditionally eat (sweet) pie for breakfast. Apple pies in particular became deeply embedded in the history of America – associated with the old country, the new country and the pioneering spirit, and indelibly identified with the sense of nationhood and patriotic sentiment.

Australia and New Zealand

The first Europeans to make their home in Australia did so, for the most part, unwillingly. They were convicts and marines and were largely devoid of agricultural or culinary skill, coming as they did predominantly from the urban poor of the large cities spawned by the Industrial Revolution. For the urban poor, meat was a prize, and if they had it at all it was likely to be in the form of a pie bought (or stolen) from a cookshop or street trader. These first migrants came to a country ideally suited for wheat-growing and grazing, and indeed the later wave of free settlers were lured to the colony with the promise of 'meat three times a day'.

The Lord-Mayor elect of Sydney in 1972 is quoted as saying that Australia was built on 'meat pies, sausages and galvanised iron', and there is a satisfying irony in the fact that, in at least one example, he was quite literally correct. When the new Parliament House in Canberra was opened in 1927, the general public was underwhelmed by the whole event, forcing caterers to bury a massive amount of prepared food (including 10,000 pies) in the local rubbish tip. Later the same year, an administration building was erected on that particular piece of ground. The building now houses the Department of the Environment and Water Resources – which somehow seems very apt, particularly when you know that, after its completion, some 620 tons of cement intended for use in its foundations was discovered unused. The stale meat pies must have been deemed sufficient.

It seems that the country's early love affair with the meat pie was shared across all ranks. The first recorded mention of a pie in an Australian newspaper was in the Melbourne *Argus* in 1850, in an article which noted that the town councillors preferred meat pies from the local pub to the food provided in the council chambers.

Unofficial regard is one thing, but one particular style of pie called the 'pie floater' is officially recognized as a South Australian Heritage Icon by the National Trust of Australia.

A famous South Australian food icon, the pie floater.

A fine symbol, many would say – a meat pie served in a puddle of mushy peas, garnished with tomato sauce. It is indeed symbolic, if Terry Pratchett has summed it up correctly in his 'vaguely Australian' story, *The Last Continent*: 'Who is this hero striding across the red desert? Champion sheep shearer, horse rider, road warrior, beer drinker, bush ranger and someone who'll even eat a Meat Pie Floater when he's *sober?*' The affectionate esteem (accompanied as it is with a total lack of illusion) in which pies are held in Australia is best reflected in some of the slang expressions for pie. Anyone for a fly cemetery, rat coffin or maggot bag?

Australians like to fancy that they are the greatest pie consumers in the world, but that accolade may well fall to New Zealanders. Exact figures are impossible to determine – large commercial bakeries are shy of releasing their information, and mom and pop bakeries never do – so the prize may never be formally awarded. As in Australia, meat not sweet pies rule in New Zealand, and they are the traditional fast food at sporting venues. Naturally, given the country's extreme suitability for sheep-rearing, the iconic pie in New Zealand is made from mutton.

Canada

Perhaps more than for any other modern culture, Canada's heritage and history is clearly revealed through its pies. The Cape Breton 'pork' pie (page 58), porkless though it may now be, is clearly descended from the medieval European tradition. Did it come via the Scots, who escaped there in huge numbers from the dramatic social and agricultural changes of the first half of the nineteenth century? Or from the French, who may have given the island its name? Brittany (inhabited by Bretons) is an area of France famous for its butter (compared with the rest of the country where oil dominates) and pork.

Canada's French heritage is reflected linguistically at least, in two popular Quebecois pies; the *tourtière*, a double-crust meat pie especially popular on Christmas Eve, and the *cipaille* or *cipate*. The *cipaille* is a multilayered pie of meat, potatoes and pastry (the name may derive from 'six pâtés'), which is strangely similar in composition and sound to a well-known English dish called 'sea pie'.

Finally, there is one pie in Canada which is unequivocally its own, born of the hard life of Nova Scotia. It is the 'seal flipper pie'. In the early days, the seal fishermen of Nova Scotia had, in the usual way of such folk, to sell the best parts of their harvest, keeping only the unwanted scraps to feed their own families. Thus was the seal flipper pie born. It is, they say, an acquired taste.

Other Places

The pie has an indisputable European heritage, but the areas in which oil is the dominant fat have by necessity taken their

Pierre Bonnard, *The Table* (1925).

cuisine in other directions. Italy has the pizza. It may be correct that the word 'pizza' is usually translated as 'pie', but it must be understood that pizza is not pie, for the simple reason that bread is not pastry. If we allow pizza to be included as pie, we might as well call a toasted sandwich a pie, which would be ridiculous.

One does not think of pies (particularly meat pies) in association with classical French cuisine. France sits on the fat/oil cusp, with both being important in cooking, but butter being essential in classic sauces. Certainly in medieval times, food was cooked inside a crust, and we have seen how pâté refers to pastry, so that pâté de foie gras was formerly a pie of fatted goose liver. That is not to say that savoury pies cannot be found in France – there is the *quiche Lorraine* and the *tourte de la vallée* of Alsace, for example – but by and large pastries in France are of the small sweet variety and fill the same role as cakes.

The Germans and Austrians have a fine baking tradition, but they seem to have expended their energy in refining their prodigious cake repertoire. There does not seem to be an important pie tradition in those countries, where the potato is king of the savoury starches.

Further north, there are pies that reflect the cold, wheat-unfriendly climate and the strongly fish-based diet. These are the Finnish pies such as the Karelian pastries made mostly of rye flour, carbohydrate-heavy with fillings of barley or buckwheat or potato or rice, and eaten with melted butter and boiled eggs. On the same grounds as given for the pizza, the other Finnish 'pie' called *kalakukko* must be excluded as it is a rye bread 'pasty' filled with a mixture of pork, fish and bacon. Finland's old master, Russia, has its *kurniks*, or chicken pies, traditional on feast days, and *piroshki/pierogi*, closer to dumplings and deep fried or boiled.

There is one other type of pastry that we have not touched on so far, but which surely should not be neglected. It is filo pastry (the name refers to the fine 'leaves') so well known in Middle Eastern cuisine. Wrapped around a nutty filling and drenched in honey syrup, it is used to make some highly addictive pastry sweets such as baklava. Filo is not just used for tooth-achingly sweet pastries. There is one filo pastry pie that deserves special mention. It is the Moroccan pie called *b'stilla*, a sweet pigeon pie which is a legacy of the early Arab influence on pastry-making, and of the medieval tradition of sweet with meat.

Pasties

Today we think of a pasty as an eat-in-the-hand, single-serving savoury pastry in the 'turnover style', but it was not always so. A 'pasty' often meant something quite different in the past. There wasn't always a clear distinction between pies and pasties, but there was a tendency for pies containing a single piece of meat (especially venison) to be called a pasty. They were often huge. Samuel Pepys in the mid-seventeenth century refers several times to sharing a single venison pasty with several friends over several days. Mrs Mary Tillinghast in her book of *Rare and Excellent Receipts* (1690) says: 'If you make your Pasty of Beef, a Surline [sur-loin] is best; if of Mutton, then a Shoulder or two Breasts is the best. A Venison, or a Beef Pasty, will take six hours baking.' This was by no means the largest pasty – some recipes called for a bushel (36 litres volume) of flour, and up to 24 hours cooking.

Today's pasty is the working man's version, a perfect meal in the hand, easily transportable to the mines or the fields. Although they are indelibly associated with Cornwall, pasties can be found in one form or another all over Britain. One particularly superb example is the 'Bedfordshire clanger', from the English county of that name, which serves as both a main course and dessert by virtue of one end having a savoury filling, the other sweet.

Cornish pasties.

The traditional ingredients of the 'oggie', as it is called in the old Cornish language, are naturally disputed, but on some things most experts agree: the meat must be chopped, not minced, the vegetables (perhaps potato, onion and turnip) must be sliced and the ingredients are not pre-cooked before they are put in the pastry. The twisted or 'crimped' edge is traditional too, and forms the 'handle' by which it is held for eating – hence the crimp must be on the side, not the top edge. The wives of Cornish tin-miners used to mark the pastry with their husband's initials to ensure that their man got the correct lunch, and they supposedly made the pasty sturdy enough to survive if it was dropped down the mineshaft.

The miners of Cornwall took their pasty tradition to America when they migrated in droves in the nineteenth century. The tradition is alive and well in the Upper Peninsula region of Michigan and in eastern Pennsylvania, and is one of the rare examples of a savoury pie tradition in the USA.

7
Imaginary Pies

But I, when I undress me,
Each night upon my knees,
Will ask the Lord to bless me,
With apple pie and cheese.
Eugene Field

It would be foolish to say that art and literature offer us almost as great a feast of pies as has ever come out of our kitchens but, nevertheless, the pie-pickings are rich among the stories and pictures that form our cultural heritage. Our exposure to the imagery of the pie begins very early – before we ever eat them – in the form of the nursery rhymes that we learn to chant as children. Understanding is not necessary to the enjoyment of these apparently non-sensical jingles, but some infants grow up to become folklorists (and urban mythologists), certain that the rhymes of their childhood must have meaning and determined that it will be discovered and exposed. They are hampered by the fact that the oral tradition of these rhymes pre-dates the written version, possibly by centuries in some cases. Inevitably then, any explanations offered involve significant conjecture.

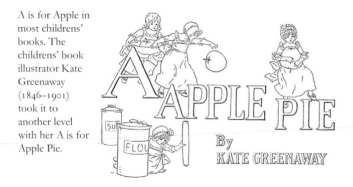

A is for Apple in most childrens' books. The childrens' book illustrator Kate Greenaway (1846–1901) took it to another level with her A is for Apple Pie.

Some interpretations are fanciful in the extreme, but usually they fall into one of two categories: they are based on historic events or people (and represent gossip or propaganda in a pre-mass media age), or they are cautionary tales for the instruction of children. The latter category probably includes the 'Three Little Kittens' (who were not going to get pie unless their lost mittens were found) and 'Simple Simon', who meets the pieman and learns, in spite of his simplicity, that a pie cannot be bought on credit.

There are two possible contenders for the real George in 'Georgie Porgie, Pudding and Pie', who kissed the girls and made them cry: George Villiers, second Duke of Buckingham (1628–1687) and the Prince Regent, the future George IV (1762–1830), both of whom were known to be amoral and gluttonous. Tradition says that 'Little Jack Horner' was based on a real person too. His real name was probably Thomas, and he was steward to the Abbott of Glastonbury during the period of the dissolution of the monasteries by Henry VIII. The 'plum' that he pulled out of the Christmas pie was the deed to the valuable manorial lands of Mells in Somerset. Depending on the version of the story you believe, he either stole the deeds which were in his safekeeping, or

The trial of the Knave of Hearts, who is accused of stealing the jam tarts by the Queen of Hearts, in *Alice's Adventures in Wonderland* by Lewis Carroll (1865).

was given them in reward for services rendered. Of course it is entirely open to conjecture whether the pie itself was metaphorical or real – for, as we have seen, sometimes pies were used to hide non-edible materials.

So what of the blackbirds baked in the pie in 'Sing a Song of Sixpence'? There are at least half a dozen interpretations

Dorothy Wheeler's depiction of the nursery rhyme 'Little Jack Horner' (1916).

An image from the Disney cartoon 'Mother Goose Goes Hollywood' (1938), in which caricatures of famous stars of the time take the place of characters in nursery rhymes. In this scene, Oliver Hardy takes the place of Pieman in the nursery rhyme 'Simple Simon met a Pieman'.

of this rhyme, some highly unlikely and some ridiculous, but it is possible that the origins of the story go back as far as 1454. In that year the Duke of Burgundy, Philip the Good, held a feast in Lille to whip up support for another crusade, and one of the entertainments was a giant pie containing a group of musicians who 'sang' when the pie was opened. The story says that there were 'eight-and-twenty' players, but a small difference in number does not destroy the theory altogether. Alternatively, the rhyme may be about the day – 24 birds representing the hours, and the opening of the pie and the singing of the birds referring to the dawn. The rhyme is certainly *not* a coded message for the recruiting of pirates, as some urban myths insist!

Inevitably, as we leave our childhood we move away from nursery rhymes to books and films, but the pie continues to appear as character, plot device, prop or metaphor in our grown-up literature. If it has not already been written, there is an entire PhD in the use and significance of the pie in Charles Dickens's works alone. Sometimes his pies are substantial icons of hospitality (the huge breakfast Yorkshire pie in *Nicholas Nickleby*), often they are 'delusive' (the pigeon pie in *David Copperfield* that is 'like a disappointing head, phrenologically speaking: full of lumps and bumps, with nothing particular underneath'), and sometimes they are vaguely sinister, like the crust full of recycled table scraps in *Our Mutual Friend* that we came across in chapter Four. The most delightful pie discussion in Dickens's work takes place in *The Pickwick Papers*:

> 'Weal pie,' said Mr Weller, soliloquizing, as he arranged the eatables on the grass. 'Wery good thing is weal pie, when you know the lady as made it, and is quite sure it ain't kittens; and arter all though, where's the odds, when they're so like weal that the wery piemen themselves don't know the difference?'

Mr Weller then goes on to repeat the advice from his pieman friend:

> "'It's the seasonin' as does it. They're all made o' them noble animals," says he, a-pointin' to a wery nice little tabby kitten, "and I seasons 'em for beefsteak, weal or kidney, 'cording to the demand. And more than that," says he, "I can make a weal a beef-steak, or a beef-steak a kidney, or any one on 'em a mutton, at a minute's notice, just as the market changes, and appetites wary!"'

A small meat pie provides more than basic nourishment in Francis Hodgson Burnett's *A Little Princess*. In the story there is an unsuitable friendship between Miss Sara and the ill-nourished, overworked little scullery maid, Becky. The kindly Miss Sara seeks out small edible treats for Becky which she hands over during their stolen moments together. On one occasion she brings some small meat pies, an amazing treat for the little maid, who enthuses, "'Them will be nice an' fillin'. It's fillin'ness that's best. Sponge cake's a 'evenly thing, but it melts away like – if you understand, Miss. These'll just stay in yer stummick.'" Becky's health visibly improves with the extra food, but she is sustained in more ways than one. She knows that 'the mere seeing of Miss Sara would have been enough without meat pies'.

The poet Louis Untermeyer wondered, 'Why has our poetry eschewed, The rapture and response of food?' Poetry has not completely eschewed the topic, but it does seem to have reserved the truly lyrical poems for luscious fruit, or very occasionally, as in the hands and heart of someone such as Pablo Neruda, for vegetables such as the tomato and onion. There are poems written about pies, but if they are not comical, the real subject is a larger theme. Robert Southey's 'Gooseberry Pie' is an ode to creation in general and to 'Jane' in particular; in John Greenleaf Whittier's poem 'Pumpkin Pie', the pie is symbolic of Thanksgiving; and the well-known quotation from the children's poet Eugene Field that forms the epigraph to this chapter comes from a poem that is a call to patriotism.

There are other opportunities for the pie to star once the medium becomes visual. They may not have featured frequently in movies, but when they do pies often steal the scene. Who could forget the role of the warm, homemade apple pie in *American Pie*? It must be the only film ever made in which the pie has a role as a sex-object.

American Pie (1999), the film that gave a whole new sexual symbolism to apple pie.

An early (1901) silent movie called *Hot Mutton Pies* played on ethnic anxieties (and revenge) with its story of two men buying and eating a pie from a Chinese vendor who, to their horror, laughs and turns his sign around to reveal the words

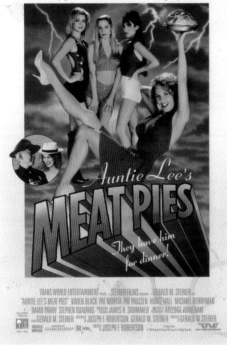

How do you handle a hungry man?

Auntie Lee's Meat Pies (1992), another story about human flesh being served up in pies to unsuspecting customers.

'Alle Samee Cat Pies'. The recurring theme of anxiety on the part of pie-eaters about the contents of pie is exploited even more graphically in *Theatre Of Blood,* a 1973 horror movie starring Vincent Price. Price plays the part of a Shakespearian actor panned by the critics who gets his revenge by murdering each of them in a very individually appropriate way. The critic Meredith Merridew (played by Robert Morley), in a scene no doubt inspired by Shakespeare's *Titus Andronicus*, chokes to death when forced to eat a pie containing his 'children' – his beloved poodles. The even greater (almost primal) fear/fascination of cannibalism is taken further in the 1992 film

Auntie Lee's Meat Pies. The theme is not new; it is straight from the eighteenth-century story of Sweeney Todd. Auntie Lee's famous pies are made with the assistance of her four beautiful nieces who find her the filling material – handsome young men.

A discussion of the pie in movies would hardly be complete without mention of the classic comic device of custard-pie throwing, now legitimized and made semi-serious as the subversive political act of 'entarting'. 'Entarting' is delivering (by 'lovingly pushing', not throwing) a cream pie into the face of a deserving celebrity, preferably in full view of the world's media, in order to make a point. It happened to Bill Gates in 1984 at the hands of the famous Belgian anarchist and

Battle of the Century (1927), which featured the biggest ever pie fight in movie history.

Desperate Dan tucking into a Cow Pie.

entarteur Noel Godin, who considers the technique a form of communication – 'a sort of visual Esperanto'. The actual message communicated does not always appear to be clear to the target or onlookers, but it is presumably so to the perpetrators, who claim to have been inspired by pie-throwing comedy movies. It is to be assumed then, that required viewing for

Waitress (2007), in which an unhappy waitress with a talent for baking vents her frustrations by inventing new pies, and ultimately thereby achieves success and happiness.

a trainee *entartiste* would be the most spectacular pie fight in movie history – the four-minute sequence from the Laurel and Hardy film *The Battle of the Century*. More than 3,000 cream pies (the entire day's production of the Los Angeles Pie Company) were ordered and not one was wasted; every one found its target, and great fun was had by all.

Finally, let us not forget cartoons. Many cartoon characters have a favourite food (Garfield has lasagne, Dagwood has huge sandwiches, Jiggs has corned beef and cabbage) but for some (Popeye and spinach for example), a particular food is essential to the storyline. Desperate Dan, the cowboy superhero from the British comic *The Dandy*, has been 'the strongest man in the world' since 1937. His great strength is attributable to his love of cow pie, which is exactly what it sounds like – a pie containing an entire cow, horns, tail and all. Sadly, after seven decades, the source of his great strength is now off the menu lest it be thought that he is promoting mad cow disease.

The online cartoon *Weebl and Bob*, with their beloved pie.

On the animated graphics side, the pie-lover par excellence is the chief character in the Flash cartoon series *The Everyday Happenings of Weebl*. The cartoon, which has almost a cult following, is minimalist in every way: Weebl and his friend Bob are simple egg shapes who roll around on a magenta background speaking in short phrases to the accompaniment of music, and their minimalist everyday routine usually revolves around the search for pie.

Epilogue:
The Future of Pie

You can say this for ready-mixes – the next generation isn't going
to have any trouble making pies exactly like mother used to make.
Earl Wilson

I asked at the beginning of this book, 'Is the pie dead?' We
have better ways now to fulfil the original functions of the
pie – we have baking dishes, lunch boxes, and refrigerators.
We no longer *need* pies. But do we still *want* them?

The commercial pie seems to be alive, after a fashion.
It has hung onto its old street-food role in the face of
competition from the likes of the hot dog and the doner
kebab, and in spite of there still being as much anxiety
about its contents as there was in Chaucer's time. Some
pies, such as Christmas mince pies and the Thanksgiving
pumpkin pie have survived because they moved beyond
mere tasty calories to become powerful symbols. The ordinary, everyday homemade pie has not been so successful
or so lucky. Does it have a future in our rushed, pastry-
phobic world? Pies are a labour (or a labour of love) to
make, and we are all time-in-the-kitchen poor. On the
other hand the conveniences of modern life mean we can
buy frozen pastry and we don't even need to turn on the

Christmas mince
pies, made in the
modern way with
fruit only – unlike
in medieval times,
when meat would
have been mixed
with the fruit.

Thanksgiving pies.

Mass-produced commercial pies.

oven – we can cook our pies in bench-top pie-makers. Are we too lazy even for this?

If the pie dynasty is as I now suspect and fear, really dying, does it matter? Does anyone care? Should we simply look back with nostalgia and record its passing? Or should we try to save it? As is usual, such a question raises even more questions. I cannot save the seal and at the same time save seal-flipper pie. Would seal-flipper pie be worth saving even if it did not require the brutal deaths of baby seals? Is it right to try to save the glorious Yorkshire Christmas pie and ignore blood pie and horsemeat pie? I am pretty sure that I personally do not want to save Spam pie, but someone out else there probably does.

Surely we should try to save something that, when done well, is not only a supreme example of the art of cooking, but a dish that encapsulates humankind's entire culinary history?

Recipes

Pastry is one area of cookery in which accurate measurement is important. In earlier times – as Gervase Markham noted in 1615 – it was assumed that the cook would know 'what paste is fit for every meate', and so a pastry recipe was not given for every type of pie.

The modern cook can get away with one recipe – for a basic shortcrust – for most pies. A few enthusiasts may tackle their own puff pastry but a good frozen brand is perfectly acceptable. Almost no one makes their own filo pastry, for obvious reasons, but almost everyone should try a hot-water crust at least once: it causes nowhere near as much anxiety as other forms of pastry.

Basic Shortcrust Pastry

The basic formula is half the amount (by weight) of fat to flour, with just enough water to bind, taking care to keep everything cool and handle as little as possible.

The following amount is sufficient for a double-crust 8-inch (20-cm) pie:

Ingredients
8 oz / 220 g plain flour, sifted

a pinch of salt
4 oz / 110 g fat (butter or a mixture of butter and lard)
2–4 tablespoons of cold water

Rub the fat into the flour and salt (or briefly pulse in a blender) until it resembles breadcrumbs. Add the water and mix quickly and lightly with the blade of a knife. When the dough starts to come away from the sides of the bowl, pat it gently together with your fingers. Wrap in plastic wrap and refrigerate for at least half an hour. Refrigerate again, if you can, for another half an hour after rolling and before cooking.

Hot-water Crust

This is suitable for the more robust type of meat pie or pasty. This amount is sufficient for four good-sized pasties.

Ingredients
10 oz / 400 g plain flour and a good pinch of salt, sifted
4½ oz / 125 g lard or dripping
(can substitute half butter for flavour)
5 fl. oz / 150 ml milk or milk and water

Place the milk and fat in a saucepan and bring to the boil. Add to the flour and mix just until it is smooth. Cut into four and roll each out into a round (about ¼-inch or ½ cm thick) while it is still warm. Fill as desired.

Cornish Pasty

Ingredients
shortcrust or other pastry made with 1 lb / 450 g flour
¾ lb / 340 g beef cut into small dice (not minced)
1 onion, finely chopped
1 piece of swede or turnip (raw) cut into small dice

2–3 raw potatoes, cut into small dice
beaten egg for glazing (optional)

Roll out the pastry to about ¼ inch thick and cut into rounds (whatever size you wish). Mix the remaining ingredients gently and pile onto one half of each round (if you want the seal along the edge) or in the centre (if you want to make the seal along the top). Damp the edges and crimp together. Brush with the beaten egg if you wish to have a glazed finish. Bake in a moderate oven for 35–45 minutes.

Stargazy Pie

Ingredients
6 to 8 pilchards
1 medium-sized onion
3 rashers of bacon
1 lemon
2 free-range eggs
18 oz / 500 g shortcrust or flaky pastry
salt and pepper to season (sea salt for greater authenticity)
parsley and tarragon for flavouring

Cornish Fish Recipe Method
Gut, clean and bone the fish, leaving on the heads and tails (you may find the flesh is so fresh you can pull the backbone free without a knife). Finely chop the onion. Chop the bacon into squares. Cut the lemon in half; set two slices to one side for decoration. Squeeze and save the juice. Finely grind the rind. Boil the eggs until soft, then cut into small dice.

Cut the pastry mixture into two halves. Roll them out and place one half in an 8-inch shallow pie dish. Cut off the overlapped edges. Coat the edge with either milk or water to ensure the pastry lid will stick.

Then either: carefully place your pilchards into the bottom of the dish arranging them, like the spokes of a wheel, around the edge of your dish. Place the mixed chopped onion, eggs and bacon in the gaps between the fish. Some recipes suggest stuffing them with half the finely chopped mixture, but given the small gut of the pilchards, is it worth trying to do so? Add the lemon juice and cover with your pastry lid, pressing down around the fish to seal the pie, trim the edges of overlapping pasty and crimp the edges in true Cornish style.

Or (and we find this more authentic): place all your chopped ingredients, including seasoning, into the dish. Cover with the pastry lid, trim the edges of overlapping pasty, crimp as above, then carefully cut slits into the pasty, hold open with the blade of a knife and gently push the whole fish into the slots, leaving just the heads or tails showing. Add the lemon juice and then seal the slits. Coat the now completed pie with beaten egg.

Cooking your Pie

Place in the middle of a pre-heated oven (200°C) for around 30 minutes, until golden-brown. (For larger pies more time might be needed.) Serve piping hot with a sprig of parsley garnish and Cornish new potatoes.

Historical Recipes

It can be a frustrating experience for a modern cook to try to reproduce historic recipes. Old cookbooks are difficult to follow because they rarely contain exact measurements or temperatures, and the instructions are very vague. The older the cookbook, the more this applies – and often the old language is also incomprehensible. Cookbooks in medieval times were not primarily written as instruction manuals – cooks learned on the job, were not expected to need books and, in any case, were not necessarily literate. They were written as *aides-memoires* for others in the household who were responsible for provisioning the kitchen, or to be included in the master's library as an indication of his wealth. It was not until the mid-nineteenth century that cookbook instructions started to become more detailed and accurate: for most historic recipes we must make educated guesses and use our own judgement. I invite you to do this with the following recipes:

Tart de Bry
—from the Master-Cooks of King Richard II,
The Forme of Cury, c. 1390

Take a Crust ynche depe in a trape. take zolkes of Ayren rawe & chese ruayn. & medle it & þe zolkes togyder. and do þerto powdour gyngur. sugur. safroun. and salt. do it in a trape, bake it and serue it forth.

NOTE: 'Bry' appears to refer to the region where this cheese tart originated: the specific cheese mentioned is 'ruayn', which was a soft autumn cheese. Because the amount of sugar is not specified in the recipe we don't know how sweet this tart was intended to be – but as sugar was very expensive at the time, it seems reasonable to assume that this was closer to what we would now call a quiche, rather than a cheesecake.

For a tarte Of apples and orenge pilles
—from Anon., *The Good Huswifes Handmaid for Cookerie in Her Kitchen*, 1597

Take your orenges and lay them in water a day and a night, then seeth them in faire water and honey and let seeth till they be soft; then let them soak in the sirrop a day and a night: then take forth and cut them small and then make your tart and season your apples with suger, synamon and ginger and put in a piece of butter and lay a course of apples and between the same course of apples a course of orenges, and so, course by course, and season your orenges as you seasoned your apples with somewhat more sugar; then lay on the lid and put it in the oven and when it is almost baked, take Rosewater and sugar and boyle them together till it be somewhat thick, then take out the Tart and take a feather and spread the rose-water and sugar on the lid and let it not burn.

NOTE : This would have been a very extravagant dish. Oranges preserved in syrup ('orengeado') as in the first step of this recipe were a very expensive delicacy. A pie such as this – an 'orengeado pie' – was grand enough that two of her pastry-cooks each gave one to Queen Elizabeth I as a New Year gift in 1600.

An Herb Pie for Lent
—from Elizabeth Raffald, *The Experienced English Housekeeper*, 1769

Take lettuce, leeks, spinach, beets, and parsley, of each a handful. Give them a boil, then chop them small, and have ready boiled in a cloth one quart of groats with two or three onions in them. Put them in a frying pan with the herbs and a good deal of salt, a pound of butter and a few apples cut thin. Stew them a few minutes over the fire, fill your dish or raised crust with it, one hour will bake it. Then serve it up.

Pompkin [Pie]
—from Amelia Simmons, *American Cookery*, 1796

No.1 One quart stewed and strained [pumpkin], 3 pints milk, six beaten eggs, sugar, mace, nutmeg and ginger, laid into paste No.7, or 3, cross and chequer it, and bake in dishes three quarters of an hour.
No.2 One quart of milk, 1 pint pompkin, 4 eggs, alspice and ginger in a crust, bake one hour.
No.7 paste ['A Paste for Sweet Meats']

Rub one third of one pound of butter, and one pound of lard into two pound of flour, wet with four whites well beaten; water as much as necessary: to make a paste; roll in the residue of shortening in ten or twelve rollings – bake quick.

NOTE : This was the first cookbook to be printed in America. The recipe appears in her 'pudding' chapter. She also has a recipe for a 'potatoe' pie – using sweet potato.

Curry Pie of Fish or Meat
—from A Lady, *Domestic economy, and cookery, for rich and poor*, 1827

The curry ought always to be prepared for pies and cooled, or much better if dressed the day before, or any left curry will answer better than one newly made; put it into a nice puff paste covered with a thin cover, set round closely with long leaves, with the points upwards, and a deep border round, with leaves falling down from the top. A pastry formed in this way is very handsome.

Plain boiled rice and curry sauce, or curried rice, must be served with it.

A Good Apple Tart
—from Eliza Acton, *Modern Cookery in All its Branches*, 1845

A pound and a quarter of apples weighed after they are pared and cored, will be sufficient for a small tart, and four ounces more for one of moderate size. Lay a border of English puff-paste, or of cream-crust round the dish, just dip the apples into water, arrange them very compactly in it, higher in the centre than at the sides, and strew amongst them from three to four ounces of pounded sugar, or more should they be very acid: the grated rind and the strained juice of half a lemon will much improve their flavour. Lay on the cover rolled thin, and ice it or not at pleasure. Send the tart to a moderate oven for about half an hour. This may be converted into the old-fashioned creamed apple tart, by cutting out the cover while it is still quite hot, leaving only about an inch-wide border of paste around the edge, and pouring over the apples when they have become cold, from half to three-quarters of a ping of rich boiled custard. The cover divided into triangular sippets was formerly stuck around the inside of the tart, but ornamental leaves of pale puff-paste have a better effect. Well-drained whipped cream may be substituted for the custard, and be piled high, and lightly over the fruit.

Apple Strudel

—from Florence Kreisler Greenbaum,
The International Jewish Cook Book, 1919

Into a large mixing bowl place one and one-half cups of flour and one-quarter teaspoon of salt. Beat one egg lightly and add it to one-third cup of warm water and combine the two mixtures. Mix the dough quickly with a knife; then knead it, place on board, stretching it up and down to make it elastic, until it leaves the board clean. Now toss it on a well-floured board, cover with a hot bowl and keep in a warm place. While preparing the filling lay the dough in the centre of a well-floured tablecloth on the table; roll out a little, brush well with some melted butter, and with hands under dough, palms down, pull and stretch the dough gently, until it is as large as the table and thin as paper, and do not tear the dough. Spread one quart of sour apples, peeled and cut fine, one-quarter pound of almonds blanched and chopped, one-half cup of raisins and currants, one cup of sugar and one teaspoon of cinnamon, evenly over three-quarters of the dough, and drop over them a few tablespoons of melted butter. Trim edges. Roll the dough over apples on one side, then hold cloth high with both hands and the strudel will roll itself over and over into one big roll, trim edges again. Then twist the roll to fit the greased pan. Bake in a hot oven until brown and crisp and brush with melted butter. If juicy small fruits or berries are used, sprinkle bread crumbs over the stretched dough to absorb the juices. Serve slightly warm.

NOTE : Is apple strudel a pie? Why not? It is encased in pastry, although not in a shaped dish, so it has the same qualifications as a pasty, does it not?

Beef-Steak and Kidney Pie
—from E. Carter, *The Frugal Cook*, 1851

Beat your steaks well, in order to make them eat tender, add one-third the weight of kidneys, cut small in order to extract all the gravy, and season with pepper and salt; line the sides and edge of the dish with paste, cover the whole with your crust, and ornament it as directed for meat pies.

NOTE: Meat and kidney have been used in pies for centuries, but the phrase 'steak and kidney pie' was not in common use until the late nineteenth century. Mrs Beeton (1861) give a recipe for steak and kidney pudding, but the only additions suggested for her basic beef-steak pie are oysters, mushrooms or minced onions. Oysters had been a traditional ingredient in 'beef' pies for centuries, and in Mrs Beeton's day were cheap food, affordable for the poor. It is probable that kidney became the common substitute when oysters started to become expensive as the Victorian era wore on.

Lamb and Currant Pie
—from Cassell's *Dictionary of Cookery*, c. 1875

Cut about two pounds of the breast of lamb into small, neat pieces. Put them in a pie-dish, and sprinkle over them a desert-spoonful of salt, a teas-spoonful of pepper, a tablespoon of finely-minced parsley, a quarter of a nutmeg, grated, and three table-spoonfuls of picked currants. Beat two eggs thoroughly, mix with them a wine-glassful of sherry, and pour them over the meat. Line the edges of the dish with a good crust, cover with the same, and bake in a moderate oven. A little white wine and sugar should be sent to the table with this pie. Time, an hour and a half to bake. Probable cost, 2s. 8d., exclusive of the wine. Sufficient for four or five persons.

NOTE : This pie with its mix of dried fruit and lamb, and the addition of sugar and wine at the table, harks back to medieval times.

Almond Tartlets
—from Theodore Francis Garrett, *The Encyclopaedia of Practical Cookery*, *c.* 1891

Line a dozen tartle-moulds with paste, but the paste on the rims of the moulds, then mask the bottom with a thin layer of marmalade. Pound 6 oz. of blanched Almonds, dried in the oven, mixing up by degrees the same amount of fine sugar, a little orange or lemon zest, and the yolks of six eggs. Remove this from the mortar, put it into a kitchen basin, and work up with it eight whipped whites of eggs. Fill the tartlets, sprinkle them over with fine sugar, and bake in a slack oven for twenty-five to thirty minutes.

Squab pot pie, à l'Anglaise
—from Victor Hirtzler, *The Hotel St. Francis Cookbook, c.* 1919

Roast the squabs and cut in two. Fry a thin slice of fillet of beef on both sides, over a quick fire, in melted butter. Put both in a pie dish with a chopped shallot that was merely heated with the fillet, six heads of canned or fresh mushrooms, one-half of a hard-boiled egg, a little chopped parsley, and some flour gravy made from the roasted squab juice, and well seasoned with a little Worcestershire sauce. Cover with pie dough and bake for twenty minutes. This is for an individual pie; make in the same proportions for a large pie.

Prune and Raisin Pie
—from Florence Kreisler Greenbaum,
The International Jewish Cook Book, 1919

Use one-half pound of prunes, cooked until soft enough to remove the stones. Mash with a fork and add the juice in which they have been cooked; one-half cup of raisins, cooked in a little water for a few minutes until soft; add to the prune mixture with one-half cup of sugar; a little ground clove or lemon juice improves the flavor. Bake with two crusts.

Lemon Cream Pie
—from Mrs C. F. Level and Miss Olga Hartley,
The Gentle Art of Cookery, 1925

One cup of sugar, one cup of water, one raw potato grated, juice and grated rind of one lemon. Mix all the ingredients together and bake in pastry top and bottom.

Egg and Bacon Pie
—from Vicomte de Mauduit, *The Viscount in the Kitchen*, 1933

This is a Yorkshire dish par excellence.

Line a pie dish with flaky pastry, cover the bottom with two layers of lean bacon, and break carefully three eggs over them. Salt and pepper, then put the dish uncovered in a hot oven. When the eggs have set, put over them two more layers of bacon, and over this break three more eggs. Pepper, cover with pastry, egg it, and bake in the hot oven till the pastry is cooked.

Vegetable Pie
—from Baron Brisse, *366 Menus and 1200 Recipes*, originally published in France in 1868; this recipe is from the 1896 English translation.

Cook some green peas, young broad beans, small carrots, and tender French beans, separately, in cream sauce; place in a baked pie-case, divided into compartments with thin pieces of paste, and serve. In winter preserved vegetables may be used for the pie. We have to thank the celebrated Grimod de la Rèyniere for inventing this dish, which not only pleases the palate but the eye, and is a great addition to our fast-day dinners.

Select Bibliography

Albala, Ken, *Food in Early Modern Europe* (Westport, CT, 2003)

David, Elizabeth, *English Bread and Yeast Cookery* (London, 1979)

Davidson, Alan, *The Oxford Companion to Food* (Oxford and New York, 1999)

Drummond, J. J., and Anne Wilbraham, *The Englishman's Food* (London, 1958)

Fernandez-Armesto, Felipe, *Food: A History* (London, 2001)

Flandrin, Jean-Louis and Massimo Montanari, *Food: A Culinary History*, trans. Albert Sonnenfeld (New York, 1999)

Hartley, Dorothy, *Food in England* (London, 1954)

Heiatt, Constance B., *An Ordinance of Pottage* (London, 1988)

Hess, L. John and Karen, *The Taste of America* (New York, 1977)

Kiple, Kenneth F. and Kremhild Coneè Ornelas, *The Cambridge World History of Food*, vols I and II (Cambridge and New York, 2001)

Larousse Gastronomique (New York, 2001)

Root, Waverley, *Food* (New York, 1980)

Shephard, Sue, *Pickled, Potted and Canned* (London, 2000)

Stewart, Katie, *Cooking and Eating* (London, 1975)

Toussaint-Samat, Maguelonne, *History of Food*, trans. Anthea Bell (Oxford, 2000)

Trager, James, *The Food Chronology* (London, 1995)

Websites and Associations

Culinary & Dietetic Texts of Europe from the
Middle Ages to 1800:
www.uni-giessen.de/gloning/kobu.htm

Gode Cookery
www.godecookery.com/godeboke/godeboke.htm

Historic Food
www.historicfood.com/portal.htm

The Food Timeline
www.foodtimeline.org/

The Historic American Cookbook Project:
http://digital.lib.msu.edu/projects/cookbooks/

What's Cooking America: History and Legends of
Favorite Foods:
http://whatscookingamerica.net/History/HistoryIndex.htm

The American Pie Council:
www.piecouncil.org/national.htm

The Melton Mowbray Pork Pie Association:
www.mmppa.co.uk/about.html

Official Great Aussie Meat Pie Competition
www.greataussiepiecomp.com.au

Acknowledgements

This book has been a great deal of fun in the making. I am delighted to have been given the opportunity to delve into and write about a topic so dear to my heart and heritage, and am honoured to be included amongst the illustrious company of the other authors in the Edible series.

My gratitude goes first to Andrew F. Smith, culinary historian and author, for recommending me for the project, to Michael Leaman of Reaktion Books for accepting me on Andrew's recommendation, and to Martha Jay for her patience with me during the post-writing production phase.

Special thanks are due to my son-in-law Patrick Bryden for his invaluable help with sourcing and preparing many of the images for this book, and to my husband Brian and our special friend Trevor Newman for managing to hold off eating the Melton Mowbray and *Pézenas* pies long enough to photograph them. I am also appreciative of the great body of loyal readers of my blog *The Old Foodie*, who have reinforced my belief that food history can be fascinating for the 'general reader' as well as the historian.

Finally, I am indescribably grateful for the unfailing support and unflagging enthusiasm of my friends and family, especially that of my husband Brian, my children (and their partners) Matthew (and Vicki) and Sarah (and Patrick), and my little sister, Val. Thank you from the bottom of my heart.

Photo Acknowledgements

The author and publishers wish to express their thanks to the below sources of illustrative material and/or permission to reproduce it. Locations of some artworks are also given below.

Accademia di Belle Arti di Brera, Milan: p. 25; photo Brian Clarkson: p. 28; photo Sandra Cunningham/shutterstock images: p. 114 (foot); photo © Janis Dreosti/2008 iStock International Inc.: p. 99; photo Everett Collection/Rex Features: p. 104; photo © Jack Jelly/2008 iStock International Inc.: p. 62; photos Library of Congress, Washington, DC: pp. 32, 36, 70, 78, 92, 115; photo © Liza McCorkle/2008 iStock International Inc.: p. 64; Maidstone Museum & Art Gallery, Kent: p. 40; photo © Monkey Business Images/shutterstock images: p. 114 (top); Musée d'Orsay, Paris: p. 34; Musée du Louvre, Paris: p. 56; photo Trevor Newman: p. 58; photo © Jeanell Norvell/2008 iStock International Inc.: p. 6; photo Roger-Viollet/Rex Features: p. 13; photo courtesy of Evan Schoo: p. 94; Tate, London: p. 96; © D. C. Thompson & Co., Ltd.: p. 11; from *The Times* (June 1945): p. 68; photo courtesy http://www.cornishlight.co.uk/: p. 79; courtesy www.weebls-stuff.com: p. 112.

Index

italic numbers refer to illustrations; **bold** to recipes